Palgrave Hate Studies

Series Editors
Neil Chakraborti
School of Criminology
University of Leicester
Leicester, UK

Barbara Perry
Faculty of Social Science and Humanities
University of Ontario
Oshawa, ON, Canada

This series builds on recent developments in the broad and interdisciplinary field of hate studies. Palgrave Hate Studies aims to bring together in one series the very best scholars who are conducting hate studies research around the world. Reflecting the range and depth of research and scholarship in this burgeoning area, the series welcomes contributions from established hate studies researchers who have helped to shape the field, as well as new scholars who are building on this tradition and breaking new ground within and outside the existing canon of hate studies research.

More information about this series at
http://www.palgrave.com/gp/series/14695

Chris Allen

Reconfiguring Islamophobia

A Radical Rethinking of a Contested Concept

palgrave
macmillan

Chris Allen
School of Criminology
University of Leicester
Leicester, UK

Palgrave Hate Studies
ISBN 978-3-030-33046-0 ISBN 978-3-030-33047-7 (eBook)
https://doi.org/10.1007/978-3-030-33047-7

This Palgrave Pivot imprint is published by the registered company Springer Nature Switzerland AG.
The registered company address is: Gewerbestrasse 11, 6330 Cham, Switzerland

It's about how hard you can get hit and keep moving forward (RB)

Acknowledgements

In some ways, this book is the culmination of nearly two decades of research into Islamophobia and a host of other associated issues. During that time, my life and the lives of those around me have changed significantly as indeed has the social and political landscape. Some things however have not changed and that is the overwhelming sense of pride and love I have for my three children—Harry, Maisie and Emily. Throughout the turmoil, they have always been most important. While it's not always easy to do so, I hope they are able to see the good and forgive the bad knowing that at all times I always had their best interests at heart.

A number of others also deserve my special thanks and recognition.

First is my good friend, former colleague and research collaborator Arshad Isakjee. I miss the many hours we spent together chatting about everything from who was behind certain Muslim organisations through to whether Millwall FC would get promoted. You really have been a major part of what I have achieved and for that reason I'll always be grateful.

The second is good friend, former colleague and research collaborator Özlem Ögtem-Young. Like Arshad, you have always been there, always championing and supporting me in whatever I have decided to do. I miss seeing you as much as I used to and not just for the free breakfasts. Without your contribution and unwavering friendship, I would not have been able to achieve what I have.

The third is Aaron Lee Langdon (Chainz). Having been friends since our days together at Birmingham Race Action Partnership (BRAP), it's nice to know that whether it's a week, a month or a year, the exact same person is always there waiting to pick up where we previously left off.

Others for whom I wish to offer my thanks to my colleagues in the Centre for Hate Studies and School of Criminology at the University of Leicester. Thanks also to Saul Becker and everyone who supported me during my 14 or so years at the University of Birmingham. A special gratitude will always be reserved for Jorgen Nielsen.

I also want to extend my thanks and gratitude to the many individuals and organisations that have supported me in one way or another over the years whether as a colleague, working with me on a project, inviting me to speak at an event, buying or reading my publications or even just sharing something I've written on social media: all are equally appreciated. The goodwill that I receive from so many people is never underestimated nor taken for granted. I hope I can continue to undertake and publish research that you find interesting and support at least some of you in your respective endeavours.

Two more thanks.

To my mum and stepdad, Ivy and Ron, and my now long-deceased grandparents, Ivy and Ernie. Through you, I never forget where I've come from or how difficult the journey from 119 Elim Estate to where I am today has been. I hope that in some ways, I've made you proud.

Finally, to Anna for being the best person to be with. Whether it's bingeing on trash TV, watching horror movies, eating out, starting our own cult or despairing at the class system, I genuinely can't think of anyone I'd rather be doing that with. Thank you for being who you are, don't ever change.

Chris.

Contents

About the Author

Chris Allen is Associate Professor of Hate Studies at the Centre for Hate Studies based in the School of Criminology at the University of Leicester. For almost two decades, he has been at the forefront of research on Islamophobia and various other issues associated with the 'problematisation' of Muslim communities. In undertaking this research, he has been funded by the Arts and Humanities Research Council, the Economic and Social Research Council, various British governmental departments, local authorities and the European Union as well as a number of different state agencies, third-sector organisations and charitable bodies. From this he has published widely in scholarly journals and collections in the UK and elsewhere around the world. Firmly committed to public engagement, he also regularly writes for a variety of non-specialist outlets, delivers talks in community and other non-academic settings and appears in the media.

Over the past decade, he has held a number of independent advisory roles across the British political spectrum including the All-Party Parliamentary Group on Islamophobia and Cross-Government Anti-Muslim Hatred Working Group. He has also contributed written and oral evidence to a number of different government bodies and commissions including the House of Lords Select Committee on Religious Offences, the All-Party Parliamentary Group on Islamophobia, All-Party Parliamentary Group on Universities, Home Affairs Select Committee on Hate Crimes and the Commission on Islam, Participation and Public Life.

Chris is a senior fellow of the Centre for Analysis of the Radical Right, a fellow of the Higher Education Academy, Royal Society of Arts, the US Department of State's International Visitor Leadership Program and an alumnus of the John Adams Society.

CHAPTER 1

Towards a Working Definition: Islamophobia and Its Contestation

Islamophobia as an academic topic of study remains relatively new, the first detailed scholarly monographs being less than a decade old (Allen, 2010; Kumar, 2012; Sheehi, 2011). As a discriminatory phenomenon afforded public and political attention, Islamophobia is slightly older. From the initial recognition of a distinct anti-Muslim discriminatory phenomenon emerging in London in the late 1980s (Allen, 2010), Islamophobia entered the public and political spaces in 1997 as a result of the ground-breaking Runnymede Trust report *Islamophobia: a challenge for us all* (Commission on British Muslims and Islamophobia, 1997). Emanating out from these embryonic origins in the context of the UK, the ensuing years have seen Islamophobia recognised in much of Europe, North America and various other places beyond. In this respect, both the term and the phenomenon of Islamophobia are firmly—and consciously—established in the lexicons of different general publics, cross-spectrum political actors and disparate disciplinary scholars. It is unsurprising then that Islamophobia has attracted the attention of the United Nations (UN). According to its Special Rapporteur on contemporary forms of racism, racial discrimination, xenophobia and related intolerance in 2008 (United Nations, 2008), given the marked increase in Islamophobia since the turn of the century, if immediate action was not taken, Islamophobia would pervade the lived experience of an ever-growing number of Muslims around the world.

C. Allen, *Reconfiguring Islamophobia*, Palgrave Hate Studies,
https://doi.org/10.1007/978-3-030-33047-7_1

In addition to its recognition, Islamophobia has also been rejected: at best, emerging as something of a contested phenomenon, and at worst, a mere construction. Routinely and regularly castigated and challenged, decried and denied, there is little evidence of Islamophobia being responded to with the certainty and seriousness afforded to it by the UN Special Rapporteur. This can be illustrated by some examples from the UK context. For example, the Quilliam foundation—a one-time UK Government-funded and London-based think tank focusing on counter-extremism that was established by former 'Islamist extremists'—claimed that merely acknowledging, let alone using, the term Islamophobia was enough to hand 'a propaganda coup to Islamists who can…present themselves as ordinary Muslims who are victims of "Islamophobia"' (Readings, Brandon, & Phelps, 2011, p. 24). So influential was this that for a number of years, the UK's coalition government ceased referring to and subsequently using the term Islamophobia, something subsequent governments have rescinded on (Allen, 2017). Beyond the political spaces, there have been a number of detractors and critics in the public spaces as well. These include the commentator Douglas Murray who cites Christopher Hitchens: 'Islamophobia is a word created by fascists, and used by cowards, to manipulate morons' (Murray, 2018). Others like the journalist Melanie Phillips concur, contesting the very reality of Islamophobia by arguing that it is little more than mere 'fiction': a 'fiction' that functions to hamper legitimate and valid criticism of Islam and Muslims (Phillips, 2018).

Despite such protestations, there exists however a vast array of evidence that not only render arguments such as Islamophobia being a mere 'fiction' as nonsense but so too prove it is unequivocally—and extremely worryingly—real. Focusing again on the UK setting, this is evident in the UK Government's official data. Noting that the level of religiously motivated hate crime has been at record highs for the past few years, Muslims comprise the majority of victims (O'Neill, 2017). In support of this, data from London's Metropolitan Police Force offers similar evidence. Focusing specifically on Islamophobic hate crimes, its data evidences increasing levels: showing a rise from 1205 Islamophobic hate crimes per year to 1678 per year most recently (De Payer, 2018). Non-official data sets suggest much the same. Tell MAMA (Measuring Anti-Muslim Attacks)—a national non-statutory organisation that offers support to Muslim victims of hate crime—has recorded year-on-year increases in the number of recorded

Islamophobic hate crimes for almost half a decade. Its most recent data shows that in the past year alone, the number of attacks increased by 30 per cent (Tell MAMA, 2017). Irrespective of critics and detractors therefore, Islamophobia is real and tangible. Far removed from those suggesting Islamophobia was conceived as a means to 'manipulate morons' or 'hamper legitimate and valid criticism', the evidence shows that Islamophobia is extremely real.

This dichotomous tension is far from the preserve of the UK. In the United States, for instance, the Southern Poverty Law Center (SPLC)—a non-profit organisation that tracks hate groups and hate crimes—claims there was a dramatic increase in the number of tangible Islamophobically motivated incidents comprising 'hateful harassment and intimidation' in the immediate aftermath of Donald Trump's election as President in November 2016 (Jones, 2016). Evidencing how this increase was sharper than following the 9/11 terror attacks, the SPLC stated that the 300 incidents it recorded in the week following Trump's election were equivalent to the number of Islamophobic incidents typically recorded in a five- to six-month period. Counter to this—and in line with the dichotomy apparent in the British setting—Trump and his supporters regularly and routinely play down the 'reality' of Islamophobia. As a report from the Bridge Institute at Georgetown University recently put it, not only is Trump's White House staffed by individuals who support discriminatory, bigoted and hateful views of Muslims and Islam, but so too does his administration legitimise and mainstream Islamophobic ideas and notions (Bridge Institute, 2017).

While data about tangible manifestations of Islamophobia is extremely limited in the Australian setting, the data that does exist illustrates that the levels of Islamophobic hate crime have been increasing since 2014 (Ozalt, 2017). Similar to the work of Tell MAMA in the UK and the SPLC in the United States, the Islamophobia Register Australia has been attempting to collate academically verified data that it too can use to evidence the realities of Islamophobia. Despite being at a relatively early stage, the data collated suggests the growing scale and prevalence of Islamophobic hate crimes across Australia. Dichotomously, the Australian media outlets have afforded platforms to those who sit in contention to the evidence at hand and who align themselves with the critics and detractors referred to previously. These have included editorial pieces in the *Sydney Morning Herald* among others that claimed Islamophobia does not exist: instead, the entire phenomenon being a mere construction that serves an ideological function (Sheehan, 2009). Sadly albeit unsurprising, this same dichotomy—one that posits evidence of a very real and tangible Islamophobia against a portfolio of arguments that seek to criticise and detract from those same realities of tangible evidence and contested concept—is also evident in Canada, France, Germany and Sweden among various others. Islamophobia's contestation—like the phenomenon itself—is truly global.

A Working Definition of Islamophobia

While there is little rationale for Islamophobia to continue to be contested in the face of overwhelming evidence of its very realities, an insight that can be extrapolated from the UK setting relates to definition; more so, the lack of an agreed definition. While on the one hand evidence shows that Islamophobia is largely akin to other forms of hate crimes that are motivated by racism, homophobia or similar (Zempi & Awan, 2016), it would seem that this is detracted from—if not entirely dismissed—by the need to convey and duly convince public and political audiences exactly what Islamophobia is and, importantly, what it is not. While considered extensively later in the book, a preliminary consideration affords not just a useful start point but so too a foundation upon which to build and develop thinking.

Despite processes of defining Islamophobia as having been something of a constant in the public and political spaces since it first entered both two decades ago (Allen, 2017), it has been the All-Party Parliamentary Group (APPG) on British Muslims that has most recently actively sought to put forward a potentially agreeable definition. As informal cross-party groups that have no official status within the UK Parliament, the APPGs are run by and for politicians albeit without precluding the involvement of individuals and organisations from outside the governmental and political spaces. Established in July 2017, the APPG on British Muslims was set up to build on the earlier work undertaken by the now defunct APPG on Islamophobia. Despite having a public remit claiming to examine a broad range of issues of importance to British Muslims, the new APPG was as much about distancing itself from the many damaging controversies that dogged—and ultimately rendered impotent—the APPG on Islamophobia as it was anything else (Allen, 2011).

Within that broad remit was a commitment by the APPG on British Muslims to investigate the prejudice, discrimination and hatred experienced by the country's Muslims. Having published reports investigating the charitable activities of Muslims in the UK (All Party Parliamentary Group on British Muslims, 2017, 2018a), it was via its third report that the APPG sought to have its greatest impact. Launched in November 2018, *Islamophobia defined: the inquiry into a working definition of Islamophobia* (All Party Parliamentary Group on British Muslims, 2018b) hoped to make history by putting forward a working definition of Islamophobia that would be adopted and subsequently acted upon by the British Government among others. Setting out how its definition was the culmination of two years of consultation and evidence gathering, it claimed its definition took in the views of academics, lawyers, local and nationally elected officials as well as Muslim organisations, activists, campaigners and local Muslim communities. Echoing the 1997 Runnymede Trust report (Commission on British Muslims and Islamophobia, 1997) two decades earlier, the APPG claimed the time was right to 'give meaning to the word and nature of the thing we call Islamophobia' (All Party Parliamentary Group on British Muslims, 2018b, p. 8).

In doing so, the APPG on British Muslims proposed the following definition: 'Islamophobia is rooted in racism and is a type of racism that targets expressions of Muslimness or perceived Muslimness' (All Party Parliamentary Group on British Muslims, 2018b, p. 11). Roundly supported by various Muslim organisations as also British-based scholars, some of those close to the APPG expressed a hope that like the working definition of anti-Semitism put forward by the International Holocaust Remembrance Alliance (IHRA), its definition would be adopted by governmental and non-governmental organisations worldwide. Its priority however was to get the UK Government to adopt it. As the report explained, this was necessary on the basis that successive British governments, individual politicians and the public had overlooked Islamophobia. This was especially evident, the APPG argued, in Islamophobia's exclusion from the Government's Hate Crime Action Plan 2017 (HM Government, 2017). Accordingly, the inference was that certain forms of discrimination were being afforded greater priority or importance than others. That the UK Government has only adopted a working definition of anti-Semitism—none exists for racism, disablism, homophobia or indeed any other discriminatory phenomena—would suggest that in the eyes of the APPG on British Muslims, the perceived problematic lack of equity was between Islamophobia and anti-Semitism.

Contesting the Working Definition

Maybe unsurprisingly, initial responses to the APPG's proposed working definition were far from unequivocal. Indicative of this was a personal email received from a local government officer who said that while they welcomed the working definition of Islamophobia, they wondered where they could find a definition of 'Muslimness'. Nonetheless, there was some positive reaction, with more than 60 British academics giving their immediate support to the proposed working definition (Allen, 2019). So too was it adopted by a number of British political parties including the Labour Party, Liberal Democrats and Plaid Cymru. Various local governments around the country also offered their support for the proposed working definition. Less positive was the response from the Conservative Party—the party of Government at the time the definition was published—which announced that it was not intending to adopt the working definition on the basis that it had 'not been broadly accepted', thereby meaning that 'further careful consideration' was necessary (Allen, 2019, p. 2). Here again, the dichotomous contestation referred to previously was once again in evidence. While so, the Government's decision not to adopt was far from surprising. As the APPG report itself noted, when asked whether a working definition of Islamophobia was necessary, the Government's Under-Secretary of State for crime, safeguarding and vulnerability—at the time Victoria Atkins MP—stated that there was no need for a definitive definition. While unequivocal, such a statement did seem to suggest that the Government—as also the political spaces more widely—had undergone a volte-face.

Other factors would also seem to have shaped the Government's decision not to adopt the APPG's proposed working definition, including voices from outside the political spaces. Among others, these included the chair of the National Police Chiefs Council—Martin Hewitt—who expressed concern that the working definition was so broad it could cause confusion among police officers tasked with enforcing it. Likewise, Hewitt claimed the definition could limit free speech, especially in relation to certain historical or theological issues. He also went on to allege that the working definition had the potential to undermine certain counter-terrorism powers (Dodd, 2019). Without supporting evidence or explanation, Hewitt's claims were—at least it would seem—premised on mere conjecture. While so, a disparate group of Christians, atheists and Sikhs, among others, expressed something similar. Including the evolutionary biologist Professor Richard Dawkins, the former Bishop of Rochester Michael Nazir-Ali, the human rights campaigner Peter Tatchell and historian Tom Holland, an open letter to the Home Secretary, Sajid Javid, stated that the working definition was too vague, and had the potential to damage free speech, curtail academic and journalistic freedom and detrimentally influence social cohesion. It added that the working definition was a covert means by which to establish a 'backdoor blasphemy law' (Allen, 2019, p. 1). What is interesting is just how similar the concerns and objections expressed here were to those previously considered by the Quilliam Foundation, Murray and Philips previously. Far from reducing the contestation, the proposed working definition would appear to have instead merely continued the same dichotomous process. In this respect, one might question the extent to which Islamophobia's contestation might ever be allayed or fully responded to.

Whether the APPG and others will continue to push the UK Government to adopt the proposed working definition of Islamophobia remains unclear at the time of writing. While the likely consequence of not adopting the working definition will be the ongoing contestation of Islamophobia, there is little evidence to suggest that adopting it would be any different. Where then does the 'problem' lie: is it that unlike other discriminatory phenomena, Islamophobia is far more difficult to define? Could it be that the 'problem' lies with the APPG's definition or indeed any other definition: have all been wholly inadequate and thereby not fit for purpose? Maybe the 'problem' lies with how those tasked with devising a definition have given too great a credence to those who seek to criticise, detract from or deny Islamophobia even exists: would any definition placate their criticisms or convince them that Islamophobia is 'real'? Or could it be that the 'problem' lies with how the process of defining Islamophobia has detracted from acknowledging the 'realities' of Islamophobia: ordinary people being targeted for hate while going about their everyday lives solely because they are—or are perceived to be—Muslim? Is it possible that the 'problem' lies in the fact that the inability to come up with an appropriate definition of Islamophobia is a mere smokescreen: a process that detracts from the fact that Islamophobia is not merely a discriminatory phenomenon but so too a highly political and politicised phenomenon. In this respect, maybe the 'problem' does not even concern definitions or the processes associated with them. How then do we navigate this impasse?

About This Book

This book responds to these—and indeed other—questions, seeking to investigate the dichotomous relationship that seems to exist between the contestation attributed to Islamophobia as a political—and public—concept and Islamophobia as a 'real' and tangible discriminatory phenomenon. While this book will consider the 'problem' referred to previously, it does not necessarily seek to offer a single or sole 'solution': the situation is far more complex. Instead, this book seeks to improve understanding about Islamophobia while arguing that the dichotomous contestation exists because it serves a number of functions. To do so, this book reframes and reconfigures existing notions and understandings of Islamophobia. This includes bridging what has been to date an unacknowledged gap between two conceptions of Islamophobia: the first, a largely uncontested discriminatory phenomenon that evidence shows is both real and tangible; and the second, a wholly problematic political phenomenon that is highly politicised, as nebulous as it is amorphous and wholly convenient. This book will do this in two ways. First, it will investigate Islamophobia as a real and tangible discriminatory phenomenon. To do so, the empirical data gathered from the testimonies of more than 100 victims of street-level Islamophobic hate crime will be analysed. Second, this book will investigate Islamophobia as a politically—and publicly—conceived phenomenon; one that is largely detached from real and tangible manifestations of Islamophobia. By consequence, so too will this require some consideration as regards the policy implications of Islamophobia. To do so, unrivalled 'insider' experience gained as an independent adviser on Islamophobia and associated issues to successive British governments, political actors, local governments and third-sector stakeholders over the past decade and a half will provide the necessary evidence. Wholly innovative and novel, this is the first time such an approach has been used to both evidence and duly investigate Islamophobia.

Accordingly, this book has a threefold structure. In Part I, key themes, methods and the existing evidence base are considered. Offering a full exposition of Islamophobia in the public and political spaces in Chap. 2, Chap. 3 does similar as regards the scholarly equivalent. Chapter 4 sets out in detail the book's unique methodological approach. Combined, this part sets out what is currently known and understood about Islamophobia while also providing the foundation upon which to unpack its complexity and contestation. It will do so through reanalysing and rethinking existing knowledge. Alongside this, full consideration will be given to the misunderstandings and misconceptions that have underpinned notions of complexity and contestation that have, in turn, also continued to detrimentally hinder meaningful responses to the phenomenon in the political, policy and public spaces whether in the UK or indeed elsewhere. Together, the chapters will also touch upon how those within the scholarly and political spaces have collectively failed to speak across the respective divides, thereby further compounding the problem. This part will also introduce the reader to existing gaps in the scholarly evidence base.

In Part II, empirical data will be drawn upon to investigate the 'realities' of Islamophobia as a tangible discriminatory phenomenon; one that is experienced by 'real' people in 'real-life' settings. In doing so, this part will explore the physical and emotional harms of Islamophobia that are experienced by individuals, families, kinship networks and communities more widely. Drawing on the first-hand narratives of victims spanning a diversity of gender, ethnic, theological and socio-economic backgrounds in different places and locations across the UK, Chaps. 5 and 6 investigate the experience of female and male victims, respectively, exploring similarities and differences as well as points of convergence and divergence. Chapter 7 builds on this by investigating those tangible manifestations of Islamophobia that target the physical structures associated with Muslims and Islam and which are known to convey a 'message'—as indeed do all forms of hate crime—to a broader audience, in this instance Muslim communities. In investigating the experience of male victims as also hate crimes that target physical structures, this book identifies gaps in the existing scholarly literature and responds accordingly. To date, both of these manifestations of Islamophobia have been peripheral, if not overlooked entirely. In sum, Part II argues and unequivocally evidences that Islamophobia is a real and tangible discriminatory phenomenon. In doing so, Part II contributes towards a better elucidation of Islamophobia that in turn allows a deeper and more meaningful understanding.

Part III investigates Islamophobia as a politically—and publicly—conceived phenomenon. Both Chaps. 8 and 9 do so through the unrivalled 'insider' experience referred to previously. Chapters 8 and 9 offer alternative political responses to Islamophobia from the perspective of the UK: Chap. 8 focusing on the approach of New Labour, and Chap. 9 the coalition and Conservative governments. Both analyse political responses to Islamophobia including various social and public policy approaches and interventions. In addition, across the two chapters, the failure to adequately respond to Islamophobia will be considered as will the failure to focus on real and tangible manifestations of Islamophobia in preference of something somewhat more vague and amorphous. In doing so, these chapters will put forward an argument that this approach is politically conducive. In doing so, these chapters will address the dichotomous tension that exists between Islamophobia as a politically conceived phenomenon and Islamophobia as a real discriminatory phenomenon. Chapter 10 draws together a number of new and innovative conclusions in the hope of reconfiguring Islamophobia in such ways that not only is the phenomenon better understood but so too might its political and public contestation be better understood and, hopefully, responded to. In doing so, this chapter—as the book's culmination—speaks across the different spaces considered in this book to offer a more meaningful way in which to understand Islamophobia and its 'realities' while simultaneously understanding how this might be meaningfully deployed to counter and challenge the seemingly unwavering criticisms and dismissals so oft employed.

In sum, this book responds to two identified needs in the existing scholarly literature and known political spaces. The first is the need for robust empirical evidence to inform and shape thinking and understanding about Islamophobia, including the need to illustrate the tangible realities of it as a discriminatory phenomenon. Doing so directly addresses the contestation evident through the exploration and consideration of real-life examples that emanate from scientifically robust social research. This will contribute new knowledge to what can be understood to be a still relatively new and embryonic scholarly canon. Second is the need for scholarly works to meaningfully communicate and respond to the confusion and complexity of thinking that is evident in the public and political spaces. Not only is the latter pressing but so too undoubtedly timely given the recent endeavours of the APPG on British Muslims to try and catalyse a political response as a means of finally addressing the phenomenon. Having engaged the APPG on Islamophobia, the APPG on British Muslims and the Cross-Government Working Group on Anti-Muslim Hate as expert advisers and submitted oral and written evidence to the House of Lords Select Committee on Religious Offences, Home Affairs Select Committee on Hate Crimes and the Commission on Islam, Participation and Public Life among others, this is an urgent and desperately needed endeavour. So too this is as urgent elsewhere given first-hand engagement with the European Union (EU), European Monitoring

Centre on Racism and Xenophobia, European Network Against Racism and being a fellow on the US State Department's International Visitor Leadership Program among others.

As regards what next, this book hopes to offer a better understanding of Islamophobia and its contestation as a means of evidencing its realities: a counterbalance to the criticisms and dismissals referred to previously. As noted about those criticisms and dismissals, they are far from the preserve of the UK. So while this book may focus on the UK, both the aims and the need of this book are much wider. What is happening—and being evidenced in the UK—is happening elsewhere too. In this way, while the evidence may be specific, the processes and problems are rather more general. Accordingly, this book speaks across national and regional borders, as indeed it does scholarly disciplines also. In doing so, this book highlights the need for new thinking as regards the public and political spaces. Speaking directly to those who work and function in those spaces, this book not only provides evidence but so too aspires to act as a rallying call: to motivate and empower like-minded individuals to come together and work towards addressing Islamophobia as a real and tangible discriminatory phenomenon. As regards the scholarly spaces, this book raises a number of new ideas that require further thinking and development. Irrespective of agreement or disagreement, these—like the gaps in the evidence that are responded to here—require greater and wider critical engagement. This book then has a radical approach with radical aspirations, both of which are much needed in the current climate.

References

All Party Parliamentary Group on British Muslims. (2017). *A very merry Muslim Christmas*. London: All Party Parliamentary Group on British Muslims.

All Party Parliamentary Group on British Muslims. (2018a). *Faith as the fourth emergency service: British Muslim charitable contributions to the UK*. London: All Party Parliamentary Group on British Muslims.

All Party Parliamentary Group on British Muslims. (2018b). *Islamophobia defined: The inquiry into a working definition of Islamophobia*. London: All Party Parliamentary Group on British Muslims.

Allen, C. (2010). *Islamophobia*. Farnham: Ashgate.

Allen, C. (2011). *A momentous occasion: A report on the All Party Parliamentary Group on Islamophobia and its secretariat*. London: All Party Parliamentary Group on Islamophobia.

Allen, C. (2017). Political approaches to tackling Islamophobia: An 'insider/outsider' analysis of the British Coalition Government's approach between 2010–15. *Social Sciences, 6*(3), 77.

Allen, C. (2019). *Islamophobia defined*. London: Religion Media Centre.

Bridge Institute. (2017). *A new era in American politics: The Trump administration and mainstream Islamophobia*. Georgetown: Georgetown University.

Commission on British Muslims and Islamophobia. (1997). *Islamophobia: A challenge for us all*. London: Runnymede Trust.

De Payer, R. (2018). Revealed: Anti-Muslim hate crimes in London soared by 40% in a year. *The London Standard*. Retrieved from https://www.standard.co.uk/news/crime/revealed-antimuslim-hate-crimes-in-london-soared-by-40-in-a-year-a3775751.html

Dodd, V. (2019). Police chiefs in row over definition of Islamophobia. *The Guardian*. Retrieved from https://www.theguardian.com/news/2019/may/15/police-chiefs-in-row-over-definition-of-islamophobia

HM Government. (2017). *Action against hate, the UK government's plan for tackling hate crime – 'Two years on'*. London: HMSO.

Jones, J. (2016). There have been more than 300 reported hate incidents since election day. *Think Progress*. Retrieved from https://thinkprogress.org/300-hate-incidents-since-election-day-bf9fd91edbd6/#.43wykakta

Kumar, D. (2012). *Islamophobia and the politics of empire*. New York: Haymarket Books.

Murray, D. (2018). The Islamophobia 'problem'. *The Spectator*. Retrieved from https://blogs.spectator.co.uk/2018/11/the-islamophobia-problem/

O'Neill, A. (2017). *Hate crime, England and Wales, 2016/17: Statistical bulletin 17/17*. London: Home Office.

Ozalt, M. (2017). Islamophobia is still raising its ugly head in Australia. *The Conversation*. Retrieved from https://theconversation.com/islamophobia-is-still-raising-its-ugly-head-in-australia-80682

Phillips, M. (2018). Islamophobia is a fiction to shut down debate. *The Times*. Retrieved from https://www.thetimes.co.uk/article/islamophobia-is-a-fiction-to-shut-down-debate-wwtzggnc7

Readings, G., Brandon, J., & Phelps, R. (2011). *Islamism and language: How using the wrong words reinforces Islamist narratives*. London: Quilliam Foundation.

Sheehan, P. (2009). Islamophobia is a fabrication. *Sydney Morning Herald*. Retrieved from https://www.smh.com.au/politics/federal/islamophobia-is-a-fabrication-20141112-9fjm.html?page=-1

Sheehi, S. (2011). *Islamophobia: The ideological campaign against Muslims*. New York: SCB Distributors.

Tell MAMA. (2017). *Beyond the incident: Outcomes for victims of anti-Muslim prejudice*. London: Faith Matters.

United Nations. (2008). *Report of the Special Rapporteur on contemporary forms of racism, racial discrimination, xenophobia and related intolerance, Doudou Diène, on the manifestations of defamation of religions and in particular on the serious implications of Islamophobia on the enjoyment of all rights*. New York: United Nations.

Zempi, I., & Awan, I. (2016). *Islamophobia: Lived experiences of online and offline victimisation*. Bristol: Policy Press.

PART I

Islamophobia in Context

CHAPTER 2

A Fear or Phobia: Islamophobia in Public and Political Context

By focusing in the opening chapter on the recent attempt by the APPG on British Muslims to propose a working definition, it is possible to consider some of the challenges faced when trying to conceive and define Islamophobia in the political—and by consequence, public—spaces. This chapter investigates this further, in particular the process of conception and definition in more detail. Accordingly, Islamophobia as both political and public phenomenon is considered. In doing so, this chapter traces the emergence and development of Islamophobia from its origins in the public spaces inhabited by Muslim communities in north London through to its recognition and acknowledgement in the political spaces of international politics and an ever-more globalised world. As part of this, the process as also the rationale for defining Islamophobia will be considered as a means of trying to better understand the extent to which a definition—as also the process of definition—can be seen to be the previously referred to 'solution' to the 'problem'. While significant emphasis will be placed on the British context—not least because it was in the British public and political spaces that Islamophobia first emerged and was afforded political recognition (Allen, 2010)—this chapter will also seek to draw resonance with other geographical settings where similar processes—and equally similar contestations—are evident.

C. Allen, *Reconfiguring Islamophobia*, Palgrave Hate Studies,
https://doi.org/10.1007/978-3-030-33047-7_2

An Emergent Phenomenon

It is right to note that the phenomenon of religiously motivated discrimination and hate in the public spaces precedes the emergence of Islamophobia in the late 1980s and early 1990s. The same is true of the political spaces also, with political engagement predating the latter years of the twentieth century. Nonetheless, it was a greater political openness to the social and civic forms of religion to have emerged since the mid-1980s in the UK (McLoughlin, 2010) and the greater impetus towards tackling inequality and discrimination that are most pertinent to considerations of Islamophobia. Driven by a need to 'do more', Jenkins and Solomos argue that while there was 'little agreement about what should be done…to help break down racially discriminatory barriers' (1989, p. 3) at the national level, the same was far from true at the local and regional equivalent. This was particularly evident in the urban conurbations where those on the political left were engaging with strategies designed to tackle what many within their rank saw as a lurch towards greater inequality and discrimination (Cooper, 2004). Rather than developing new policies and legislation, the focus was on how to extend prevailing principles of equality to those with 'new'—and at times, controversial—markers of identity. Going beyond traditional markers of identity—for instance 'race' and gender—such strategies radically challenged established views that among others, sexual orientation was more than mere conduct or behaviour. Likewise, that religion was more than a mere set of beliefs and practices. Despite only achieving a few minor breakthroughs at the national level, these newly radical strategies had an important legacy. As Cooper puts it, they unequivocally shaped and influence markers of identity were conceived and understood when applied to discriminatory phenomena (Cooper, 2004).

Excepting the Northern Irish context, political recognition of religiously motivated discrimination and hate was largely invisible in the British political spaces for much of the twentieth century. However, evidence of change became apparent in the late 1980s with calls for religious discrimination to be made unlawful in the aftermath of the *Satanic Verses* furore. For Weller (2006), the furore surrounding Salman Rushdie's novel simultaneously catalysed Britain's Muslims to act while also placing them under unprecedented scrutiny. Among others, this resulted in Muslim communities and organisations increasingly utilising religion as a marker of individual and community identity as also political advocacy and engagement. For the first time, it also placed Muslims, their communities and their organisations firmly in the public and political gaze. It was not until 1993 however when the Commission for Racial Equality (CRE) called for religious discrimination to be made unlawful that some momentum was evident. As it put it at the time, 'it is at present within the law to incite hatred against a religious community and to discriminate against a person because of their religion, unless affiliation to a religion happens to be recognised as membership of an ethnic group' (Blakemore & Drake, 1996, p. 115). In spite of this, neither the CRE nor indeed any other organisation or institution was able to substantiate the reality of religiously motivated discrimination with empirical evidence. Seen to be largely anecdotal or based on conjecture, such claims were typically dismissed out of hand within the political spaces.

The first Muslim organisation to call for protection against religiously motivated discrimination was the UK Action Committee on Islamic Affairs (UKACIA) (Allen, 2013). Emboldened by the public statements by the CRE, UKACIA followed up its campaigning with a report published in 1993. Drawing on earlier policy reforms relating to racially motivated discrimination, it called for comparative protection for religiously motivated discrimination: 'where unfair discrimination is involved, the necessity of legal remedies is now generally accepted. To fail to provide a remedy against an injustice strikes at the rule of law' (Weller, 2006, p. 304). As before however, UKACIA had little evidence to convince politicians and policymakers that such 'an injustice' was indeed a reality. Desperate to fill the evidence void, the CRE oversaw a survey, a year later, of agencies that received complaints of religiously motivated discrimination. Still unconvincing, not least because it received extremely low numbers of responses (Weller, 2006), an important development took place in the same year. Via the *Anti-Discrimination (Amendment) Act 1994*, levels of protection afforded to ethnic groups under the *Race Relations Act (RRA) 1976* were extended to mono-ethnic religious groups, namely Jews and Sikhs. Shortly after, two leaflets came into circulation. The first, by the Inner Cities Religious Council and titled *Challenging religious discrimination: a guide for faith communities and their advisers*; the second, from the CRE titled *Religious discrimination: your rights.* While so, neither did the newly extended legislation afford protection to Muslims—given they were multi- rather than mono-ethnic—nor did the leaflets refer to any Muslim-specific discrimination or hate.

A growing awareness of a Muslim-specific discriminatory phenomenon was however beginning to emerge in the public spaces. While much has been made of the etymology of the word Islamophobia and its first formal use (Bogacki, de Ruiter, & Sèze, 2019), by this time—and from first hand engagement—a number of Muslim activists based in north London had begun to use the term Islamophobia to describe what they and others were experiencing (Allen, 2010). It is important to contextualise this, with the Islamophobia they were experiencing referred to prejudice, discrimination, bigotry or hate specifically targeting Muslims and those perceived to be. It was only after the term was used by the *Runnymede Trust*—a British race equality think tank—that it gained broader credence and use (Commission on British Muslims and Islamophobia, 1997). Having previously appeared in a report published on behalf of the Runnymede Commission on anti-Semitism (1994), the report noted that in common with the levels of discrimination and hate being experienced by Britain's Jews, so too were levels of discrimination and hate targeting Britain's Muslims rapidly increasing. This was the first time—albeit unsubstantiated—that Islamophobia and anti-Semitism were considered to be similar. While the report failed to evidence the Islamophobia it referred to, it nonetheless catalysed the Commission on British Muslims and Islamophobia (CBMI). A few years later and once again in collaboration with the *Runnymede Trust*, the CBMI published its report. Titled *Islamophobia: a challenge for us all* (Commission on British Muslims and Islamophobia, 1997), it sought to reach and speak directly to the newly elected New Labour Government.

A Challenge for Us All

Undoubtedly and unequivocally groundbreaking, the CBMI report not only afforded political recognition to the phenomenon of Islamophobia but so too conferred legitimacy on it. Whether in the UK or elsewhere, the significance and impact of the CBMI report in placing the phenomenon of Islamophobia in the political spaces should neither be underplayed nor underestimated (Allen, 2010). Calling for 'decisive action', the report proposed 60 multi-sector interventions few of which were subsequently actioned by neither the incoming New Labour Government or any other government since. Despite being groundbreaking, the lack of success in prompting decisive action renders both the report and CBMI failures (Allen, 2010). Whether consequential or not, the incoming Labour Government did however not only go on to acknowledge religion within the political spaces but so too designed a number of political interventions that had religion at the centre. These will be explored in greater depth in Chap. 8.

While it might be right to question the impact of the CBMI report in the political spaces, its definition of Islamophobia had significant impact; in many ways shaping and informing how Islamophobia has been conceived and defined since. That definition posited Islamophobia as 'a useful shorthand way of referring to the dread or hatred of Islam…and, therefore, to fear or dislike all or most Muslims' (Commission on British Muslims and Islamophobia, 1997, p. 1). For it, Islamophobia was somewhat literal and thereby observable through a series of recurring characteristics referred to as 'closed views'. Among others, these closed views conceived Muslims—and importantly, the religion of Islam—as an enemy, as violent, aggressive, threatening, separate and 'other'. The report also, somewhat inappropriately, deemed criticisms and dismissals of Islamophobia a 'closed view'. Overly simplistic and completely uncritical, much has been made of the problematic nature and inherent flaws in both definition and closed views. As Allen (2013, 2017) variously notes, if the 'closed views' equate to Islamophobia, then any opposite 'open views'—also set out in the report—equate to Islamophilia: an equally unwelcome and unwarranted phenomenon as Islamophobia itself.

This established a dangerous precedent for critics and detractors. For them, the definition and closed views made it extremely easy—and convenient—for those and those likeminded, to deploy allegations of Islamophobia as a shield behind which to deflect or dismiss all criticism and questioning of Muslims and the religion of Islam irrespective of legitimacy. Similarly, they argued that behind the drive to tackle Islamophobia was a far more pernicious agenda: one seeking to impose Islamophilia as the norm (Allen, 2010). Aside from these however—and not least because of fears about their motivations for criticising the definition and closed views characterisation—the CBMI's approach did negate the necessary nuance and complexity that sits between such binaries. Consequently, it conceived Islamophobia in ways that were patronising and inauthentic (Allen, 2010). Yet in spite of this, the CBMI definition has been widely and uncritically endorsed and adopted across a range of settings and contexts. For Allen (2013), not only is this widespread and uncritical adoption key to the failure to effectively communicate what Islamophobia is—and importantly, is not—but so too is it why politicians and policymakers were at least initially left unconvinced about the necessity for a response.

Beyond Britain, Enter Europe

Within a few years of the CBMI report's publication, its reach and impact beyond the UK were readily apparent. First evidence of this was in the research of the European Monitoring Centre on Racism and Xenophobia (EUMC) into Islamophobia in the European Union (EU) in the immediate aftermath of the 9/11 terror attacks (Allen & Nielsen, 2002). In addition to evidencing a backlash against Muslims in each of the then 15 member states, the EUMC also investigated how different member states duly defined Islamophobia in relation to political or policy interventions. From doing so, 7 of the 15 (Denmark, Finland, Germany, Greece, Italy, Luxembourg and Portugal) were found to have no clear or operable definition. Of the remaining eight, three quoted the CBMI (Austria, Ireland and the UK) while two more alluded to it without formally attributing it (France and the Netherlands). Only Belgium, Spain and Sweden offered definitions that were not the CBMI's (Allen & Nielsen, 2002). While it is interesting to note how rapidly the notion of Islamophobia spread beyond the political spaces of the UK, it is equally interesting to note how rapidly the CBMI's largely literal, flawed and overly simplistic definition of the same not only spread but so too filled the void as regards evidential knowledge and critical understanding.

In spite of this, the *EUMC* refrained from positing its own definition of Islamophobia, at least initially. Instead, it alluded to Islamophobia being akin to racism and xenophobia (Allen & Nielsen, 2002). In this respect, the ensuing report left open to interpretation exactly what Islamophobia was and was not. That Islamophobia was new, seemingly spreading and becoming more virulent, and importantly, largely undefined one might question the EUMC's rationale not to define the phenomenon or at least offer institutional steer. An explanation if not a rationale did however become apparent a few years later, in its 2007 report *Muslims in the European Union: Discrimination and Islamophobia* (European Monitoring Centre on Racism and Xenophobia, 2007). While acknowledging the impact of the CBMI in raising awareness of Islamophobia in the political spaces of Europe, the EUMC was however largely critical. As it explained, the CBMI definition—for the EUMC at least—was too loose and thereby too broadly applied hence why it did not use it at the time. In hindsight, the EUMC believed that it was far more meaningful to conceive and define Islamophobia as a form of racism (European Monitoring Centre on Racism and Xenophobia, 2007). It is worth noting that this extremely similar approach to the proposed working definition of the APPG on British Muslims predated it by more than a decade. In this respect, the APPG's definition was neither new nor without precedent. For the EUMC, Islamophobia—like racism—took on many guises. As it went on, these guises comprised a broad spectrum that ranged from negative general attitudes through to acts of harassment and violence (European Monitoring Centre on Racism and Xenophobia, 2007). This was the first time a tension was evident in the political spaces as regards how to conceive and define Islamophobia: a phenomenon akin to racism or one akin to a fear and thereby a phobia more literally.

A year before this, the Council of Europe (2005) had posited a definition of Islamophobia. Acknowledging it was not easy to understand Islamophobia let alone respond to it; the Council nonetheless positioned Islamophobia unequivocally within the context of racism and racial discrimination. For it, constructions of 'race' and manifestations of racism took multiple forms, many seemingly disconnected from traditional and historical notions and understandings of what constitute both. Accordingly, it was right to understand Islamophobia as a form of racism albeit one that took on certain religious and 'civilisational' connotations. Accordingly:

> *Islamophobia can be defined as the fear of or prejudiced viewpoint towards Islam, Muslims and matters pertaining to them…characterised by suspicion, deep-rooted prejudice, ignorance, and, in some cases, physical and verbal harassment. Whether it takes the shape of daily forms of racism and discrimination or more violent forms, Islamophobia is a violation of human rights.* (Council of Europe, 2005, p. 6)

While broad, the definition offers a number of advantages over the CBMI's. Most notable was the Council of Europe's attempt to emphasise the unexceptional nature of Islamophobia, evident in how it is manifested and expressed in 'daily forms' of discrimination and violence. Unlike the CBMI, the Council of Europe's Islamophobia is far from unfounded and exceptional; instead, it is founded and normal and for that reason, extremely problematic.

Going Global

As noted in the preceding chapter, similar to how the notion of Islamophobia rapidly spread to other European countries and contexts, so too did the need to define it go global. According to the UN Special

Rapporteur on contemporary forms of racism, racial discrimination, xenophobia and related intolerance, one of the reasons for this was the marked increase in the levels of Islamophobia evident since the turn of the century (United Nations, 2008). In seeking to define Islamophobia then as a global phenomenon, the following was offered:

> *[Islamophobia] refers to a baseless hostility and fear vis-à-vis Islam, and as a result a fear of and aversion towards all Muslims or the majority of them. It also refers to the practical consequences of this hostility in terms of discrimination, prejudices and unequal treatment of which Muslims (individuals and communities) are victims and their exclusion from major political and social spheres. The term was invented in response to a new reality: the increasing discrimination against Muslims which has manifested itself in recent years.* (United Nations, 2008, p. 8)

This definition can be seen to be markedly different from that of the EUMC and Council of Europe: most apparent in the lack of explicit link between Islamophobia and racism. There are two other significant differences. The first relates to the inference that Islamophobia is not new. While the definition refers to a 'new reality', the UN Special Rapporteur noted that 'Islamophobia is not a new phenomenon, dating as it does from Islam's earliest contacts with other religions and cultures, in particular the encounter with the Christian world' (United Nations, 2008, p. 8). Whether Islamophobia is a new and contemporary phenomenon or a constant and thereby historical one is important and one that is considered more fully in the next chapter. The second is how the UN Special Rapporteur refers to Islamophobia in the context of defamation of religion, specifically the defamation of Islam. If a straightforward understanding of defamation is a statement that harms reputation, the UN Special Rapporteur's definition is significantly and unequivocally different from other definitions posited in the political spaces.

Defamation of religion, in particular the defamation of Islam does find form in another definition at the global level. Soon after the UN Special Rapporteur posited its own interpretation, the Organisation of Islamic Cooperation (OIC) put forward its. The second largest inter-governmental organisation after the UN with a membership in 57 different states in 4 different continents, the OIC's definition made no distinction between the discrimination and—as it put it—intolerance shown towards Muslims and the defamation of Islam. As it stated in its first Islamophobia Observatory report, Islamophobia is:

> *an irrational or very powerful fear or dislike of Islam and the feeling as if the Muslims are under siege and attack…[going] much beyond this and incorporates racial hatred, intolerance, prejudice, discrimination and stereotyping. The phenomenon of Islamophobia in its essence is a religion-based resentment.* (Organisation of Islamic Cooperation, 2008, p. 8)

Like the CBMI, not only is the OIC definition grounded in fear and thereby a dislike also, but so too does that fear—and all that ensues from it—centre on the religion of Islam for whom Muslims, the definition adds, experience the tangible consequences. Another largely literal interpretation, many of the same criticisms and flaws evident in the CBMI definition are evident in the OIC's.

Definitional Tensions

While the constraints of this text do not allow for a full consideration of every definition of Islamophobia posited in the political spaces of each national, regional and international setting, those considered here are nonetheless indicative. From this viewpoint, two broad categories of definition emerge. The first conceives and defines Islamophobia as being akin to racism in ideology, expression and manifestation and is specifically targeted at Muslims and their communities or those perceived to be. The second conceives and defines Islamophobia as akin to a phobia from which fear and dislike duly emanate, primarily targeting the religion of Islam that in turn has detrimental consequences for Muslims and their communities. That these two categories rarely overlap highlights another dichotomy as regards Islamophobia and the process of defining it in the political and by extension, public spaces. While the two are far from mutually exclusive—at times, racism being premised by a perceived or wholly irrational fear or dislike—in the context of the political spaces, this is rarely if indeed ever acknowledged. One reason why this might be so is because of a lack of understanding about why a definition is important and the function such a definition might ultimately serve. From analysing different political settings and contexts, there is little evidence of this aside from somewhat vague notions and statements about promoting a 'better understanding'.

This is true of the British setting where a similar tension between the two categories of definition is readily apparent. In this respect, that tension is evident in the disparity that exists between the data evidencing Islamophobia as a tangible phenomenon experienced by individuals going about their everyday lives and the intangible refusal by critics and detractors to acknowledge the very existence of that same Islamophobia. This tension is also evident in the reluctance by the UK Government to adopt the APPG on British Muslims' proposed working definition. Given the embeddedness of the CBMI definition in the British political setting—despite its known and inherent flaws—the working definition's insistence on Islamophobia being 'a type of racism' not only illustrates that tension but so too the lack of overlap let alone understanding that exists in the political spaces. Here again, it is necessary to return to the question why a definition is necessary. Is it to allay the concerns of critics and detractors or is it a start point from which to develop and build political mechanisms and policy interventions to respond to the growing prevalence of tangible manifestations of Islamophobia? While it is highly unlikely to have placated the former, it is also difficult to see how the proposed working definition—or indeed any definition—might support the development of the latter. Despite the process of defining Islamophobia having been a cause célèbre for almost two decades, we are as far from knowing exactly what function that definition would serve in the public and political spaces as we have ever been. So too are we as far from finding that highly elusive yet entirely necessary definition that so many seem to believe will immediately and unequivocally provide the 'solution' to the 'problem' that no one really knows exactly what that is.

References

Allen, C. (2010). *Islamophobia*. Farnham: Ashgate.

Allen, C. (2013). Passing the dinner table test: Retrospective and prospective approaches to tackling Islamophobia in Britain. *SAGE Open, 3*(2).

Allen, C. (2017). Political approaches to tackling Islamophobia: An 'insider/outsider' analysis of the British Coalition Government's approach between 2010–15. *Social Sciences, 6*(3), 77.

Allen, C., & Nielsen, J. S. (2002). *Summary report on Islamophobia in the EU after 11 September 2001*. Vienna: EUMC.

Blakemore, K., & Drake, R. F. (1996). *Understanding equal opportunity policies*. New York: Prentice Hall Professional Technical Reference.

Bogacki, M., de Ruiter, J. J., & Sèze, R. (2019). Defining Islamophobia and its socio-political applications in the light of the Charlie Hebdo attacks in Paris. *Rosenberg Quarterly*. Retrieved from http://rozenbergquarterly.com/defining-islamophobia-and-its-socio-political-applications-in-the-light-of-the-charlie-hebdo-attacks-in-paris-2/

Commission on British Muslims and Islamophobia. (1997). *Islamophobia: A challenge for us all*. London: Runnymede Trust.

Cooper, D. (2004). *Challenging diversity: Rethinking equality and the value of difference*. Cambridge: Cambridge University Press.

Council of Europe. (2005). *Islamophobia and its consequences on young people*. Vienna: COE.

European Monitoring Centre on Racism and Xenophobia. (2007). *Muslims in the European Union: Discrimination and Islamophobia*. Vienna, Austria.

Jenkins, R., & Solomos, J. (1989). Racism, equal opportunity and public policy. In R. Jenkins & J. Solomos (Eds.), *Racism and equal opportunity policies in the 1980s* (pp. 3–29). Cambridge, UK: Cambridge University Press.

McLoughlin, S. (2010). From race to faith relations, the local to the national level: The state and Muslim organisations in Britain. In A. Kreienbrink & M. Bodenstein (Eds.), *Muslim organisations and the state: European perspectives* (pp. 123–149). Nürnberg, Bavaria, Germany: Bundesamt für Migration und Flüchtlinge.

Organisation of Islamic Cooperation. (2008). *1st OIC observatory report on Islamophobia*. Kampala, Uganda: OIC.

Runnymede Commission on Anti-Semitism. (1994). *A very light sleeper: The persistence and dangers of anti-Semitism*. London: Runnymede Trust.

United Nations. (2008). *Report of the Special Rapporteur on contemporary forms of racism, racial discrimination, xenophobia and related intolerance, Doudou Diène, on the manifestations of defamation of religions and in particular on the serious implications of Islamophobia on the enjoyment of all rights*. New York: United Nations.

Weller, P. (2006). Addressing religious discrimination and Islamophobia: Muslims and liberal democracies. The case of the United Kingdom. *Journal of Islamic Studies, 17*, 295–325.

CHAPTER 3

Akin to Racism: Islamophobia in Scholarly Context

The disagreement referred to in the previous chapter about whether Islamophobia is wholly contemporary is evident among scholars as well. While the majority view is that Islamophobia is contemporary, there is some divergence (Allen, 2010a). Sardar (1995), for instance, suggests Islamophobia today is a mere contemporary incarnation of a much older and longer historical phenomenon. For him, Islamophobia can be retrospectively applied to name, conceive and define all historical manifestations of bigotry and hate—as also hostility and conflict—between Muslims and Islam and its Western and Christian counterparts. Milton-Edwards (2002) alludes to something similar: contemporary manifestations being part of a historical continuum. Accordingly, contemporary and historical forms are one and the same. Hussain (2004) offers more nuance, arguing that throughout history a type of Islamophobia has been manifested that is specific to certain times and locations. Describing a 'plurality of Islamophobias', he states that each manifestation has characteristics derived from the prevailing religious, cultural, social and political circumstances relevant to the time. While there might then have been shared characteristics of Islamophobia evident throughout history, each of the pluralities are also different and thereby specific as well.

In line with Allen (2010a) and Sheehi (2011), among others, this book conceives Islamophobia as a wholly contemporary discriminatory phenomenon. While this rejects the notion that today's Islamophobia is the same as other historical phenomena—irrespective of whether that functions

C. Allen, *Reconfiguring Islamophobia*, Palgrave Hate Studies,
https://doi.org/10.1007/978-3-030-33047-7_3

as a continuum or is time and place specific—it does not deny a functional relationship between the historical and the contemporary. Halliday best articulates this: 'To identify these relics and revivals is not to prove a continuity of culture or politics...Instead, the past provides a reserve of reference and symbol for the present' (1999, p. 179). Therefore, in considering today's Islamophobia, while history cannot be ignored, it cannot be understood as providing anything more than a reserve of meanings and understandings that are variously and asymmetrically made known in order to reframe, reinterpret and re-present in ways appropriate and relevant to today's social, political, cultural and religious context. This is the premise upon which Islamophobia is understood from hereon.

Early Scholarly Definitions

As with the political spaces, the CBMI definition of Islamophobia had a significant impact on early scholarly definitions. Interpreted literally and incorporating many of the flaws and weaknesses referred to previously, Kayaoglu and Kaya (2012) are right to suggest that early definitions conceived Islamophobia as little more than a fuzzy concept. According to Shyrock, this was because these early studies were simplistic, simplified and "impervious to nuance" (2010, p. 9). Allen (2010b) agrees, arguing that this rendered Islamophobia as weak and unconvincing as it was in the academic spaces as indeed it was the public and political. Sayyid (2010) makes an important intervention however as regards differentiating the scholarly from the public and political. As regards the former—referred to as the analytical—Islamophobia was established as a nebulous and perpetually contested phenomenon. As regards the latter—referred to as the polemical—Islamophobia was locked within discourses of those venting grievances, smugly pontificating or seeking the ear of politicians and policymakers, a point pertinent to Chap. 9 and the failings of the Cross-Government Working Group on Anti-Muslim Hate. Irrespective of setting, conceptions and definitions of Islamophobia were wholly ineffectual: lacking the clear meaning necessary among those utilising it (Allen, 2010b). Routinely devoid of specificity, Islamophobia in early scholarly studies therefore relied on conjecture and conflation that in turn left it open to challenge, contestation and, ultimately, rejection (Sayyid, 2010). For Vakil (2010), this prompted the need to suspend engagement with Islamophobia as both a term and phenomenon. While so, this undoubtedly miscasts the issue.

As with political definitions, scholarly definitions rapidly expanded beyond the borders where the phenomenon first emerged and was duly acknowledged. This was particularly evident in Europe where a range of different approaches to understanding and defining began to emerge. In Austria, Hödl simplistically defined Islamophobia as 'a hostile attitude toward or hostile practices against Muslims and Islam that is accepted or embraced by large parts of the society' (2010, p. 443). In Belgium, Zemni's minimalist approach saw Islamophobia being reduced to the 'dehumanisation of Muslims' (2011, p. 39). As with political definitions, some sought to emphasise similarities with other discriminatory phenomena. In the Swiss context, Helbling (2010) did so by drawing direct comparisons with xenophobia. Kühnel and Leibold (2007) did something somewhat similar. From a Nordic perspective however, Schwarz and Cauchon (2012) disagreed. For them, Islamophobia had to be understood as being contingent on the social, political and cultural settings in which it was manifested. For them, this necessitated that Islamophobia was both distinct and different from xenophobia. Because—they argued—Islamophobia in Nordic countries was undoubtedly shaped and informed by 500 years of Lutheran-Protestant Christianity, so this was always going to be vastly and inherently different from Islamophobia in Mediterranean countries or in North America among others. For them, the past provided a reserve that shaped and informed the contemporary.

A Critical Turn

With little consensus evident, it was surprising when Klug (2012) declared that Islamophobia had 'come of age' as a scholarly topic. Two reasons for this might be suggested. First, Moosavi (2014) argues that this was because an increasing number of scholars were unequivocally stating that Islamophobia was 'real'. He added that as a result, Islamophobia should no longer be contested. Second, it was the emergence of studies that were employing a rather more critical approach to investigating Islamophobia. Going beyond Islamophobia as a 'fuzzy' concept, these studies could be easily demarcated from their overly simplistic earlier equivalent. As Allen put it, these critical studies targeted the 'grey', going beyond 'the black and white duality of the love or hate of Muslims and Islam as the only options available' to better understand 'the more indirect forms of Islamophobia that fall in between' (2010b, p. 54). Among others, these critical studies include Allen (2010a), Sheehi (2011), Taras (2012) and

Tyrer (2013). More recently published studies by Carr (2016) and Jackson (2018) as also Wolfreys (2018) are in a similar vein.

What is important about this turn in the scholarly literature is the emergence of a body of work that sought to critically and analytically conceive and define Islamophobia. And in doing so, a resonance between scholarly and politically conceived definitions of Islamophobia was apparent. In this respect, pre-critical turn studies were more literally inclined, defining Islamophobia as a fear and dislike of Islam and by consequence Muslims too. Post-critical turn studies however typically posited definitions that understood Islamophobia as being akin to racism if not necessarily a form of racism. The latter is particularly evident in the work of Carr (2016) who goes as far to argue the need for the descriptor 'anti-Muslim racism' to replace that of 'Islamophobia'. Nonetheless, what emerges is a spectrum of understanding: from Islamophobia being resonant with racism through functioning similar to it and at its extreme, being a manifestation of it. While little consensus about any given definition emerged, there was a shared consensus about how Islamophobia is best conceived as also its characteristics.

From analysing those critical turn studies, five recurring characteristics emerge. The first is that Islamophobia is neither consistent nor uniform, whereby a multiplicity of understandings and importantly definitions are evident. From the analysis however, this was not seen to be problematic. Second, there is an asymmetrical shifting between implicit and explicit identifiers and markers of being Muslim (Muslimness) or the religion of Islam that are used to identify and subsequently target Muslims for discrimination, bigotry and hate. Third, Islamophobia is shaped and influenced by meanings drawn from religious, social, cultural and racial frames to the extent that, at times, neither 'Muslim' nor 'Islam' needs naming. This is similar to when racist tropes suggest that someone does not belong because of their 'race' albeit without ever referring to it. A recent illustration of this was when President Trump told four congresswomen—Alexandria Ocasio-Cortez, Ilhan Omar, Ayanna Pressley and Rashida Tlaib—to 'go back' to their own countries despite all being American citizens (BBC News, 2019). While neither their nationality nor 'race' was stated, the mere inference was enough to make the slur function. Fourth, Islamophobia is contextual to the different national, cultural, political and geopolitical settings in which it is expressed and manifested. Islamophobia can therefore be specifically local or entirely global. Finally, Islamophobia can draw on historical incidents and legacies as much as contemporary equivalents in order to find justification and legitimacy.

Islamophobia: Rooted in Racism, a Type of Racism

As Jackson (2018) points out, when it is claimed that Islamophobia is a form of racism or akin to it, critics quickly point out that Muslims are not a 'race' and that adherence and identification with any given religion is by choice and not biologically determined. While the latter affords little credibility in scholarly studies, this argument does find form in both public and political spaces, acting—as Jackson rightly notes—as a form of a disclaimer for those seeking to criticise Muslims and the religion of Islam in ways that err suspiciously close to being Islamophobic. In the same way, the disclaimer 'I'm not a racist, but' is a trope for racists, so 'Muslims aren't a race so I can't be a racist' would appear to be something of an equivalent. This and the thinking underpinning it are problematic for two reasons. First, because the argument about the notion of choice as regards religious identity fails to take into account how discriminatory phenomena attribute religious—and other—identities, and so too the negative stereotypes linked to this process of attribution. Second, because such arguments overlook the processes of racialisation that duly ensue as regards the attribution of identities. That so many empirical studies on Islamophobia have highlighted how perpetrators target victims because of their attributed—and thereby, external—identity as opposed their piety or commitment to the practice of their religion perfectly illustrates this (Allen, Isakjee, & Ögtem-Young, 2013). For those arguing Islamophobia either as racism or akin to it, this is more about the processes of racialisation than it is an argument for perceiving Muslims to be a 'race'.

Similarly, Carr (2016) states that Islamophobia is far less about phenotypical characteristics than it is about the processes of racialisation that seek to 'other' Muslims. For him, Islamophobia occurs less in relation to the identification and subsequent targeting of phenotypical features than it does in those relating to what he refers to as markers of actual or perceived Muslimness. Deploying the descriptor prior to the APPG on British Muslims (2018), markers of Muslimness include certain forms of address and traditional attire, a factor so prevalent in the third wave of studies investigating Islamophobia, explored in more detail below. Unlike others, Carr (2016) uses this to argue the need to describe this as anti-Muslim racism, his reasons being twofold. First, because of the utility afforded by the term 'racism' and the potential to alert us to the process of racialisation that is occurring as regards perceptions of Muslimness. Second, because people typically 'get' racism and, importantly, the need to tackle it is seen as being 'common sense': something he argues is far from true in relation to Islamophobia.

Another way to consider Islamophobia as a form of racism or being akin to it is through the lens of how it functions. Drawing on theories of racism developed by Miles (1989), Miles and Brown (2003) and Wieviorka (1995), Allen (2010a) sets out three comparative components applicable to both Islamophobia and racism. First is how they are both ideologies and therefore function ideologically. Second, both comprise a certain set of prejudices, opinions and attitudes. Third, both manifest through exclusionary practices that include acts of violence and are likely to be consequential of the operationalisation of the prejudices, opinions and attitudes referred to previously. Sheehi (2011) concurs, adding that it is necessary to understand how exclusionary practices—including acts of violence—experienced in the daily lives of Muslims are located within an ideology that permeates current and contemporary political, social and cultural norms. If we fail to do so, he adds, such exclusionary practices are only ever seen to be tangential and scattered when, in fact, the deployment of those prejudices, opinions and attitudes is the resultant of new and existing relations of power and meaning (Sheehi, 2011).

For Allen (2010a), understanding Islamophobia in this way helps to 'join up' the now-established body of critical turn studies with the now-apparent 'third wave' equivalent. This third wave pertains to a series of primarily small-scale qualitative studies that variously investigate the encounter and experience of Islamophobia in the form of exclusionary practices. Narrow in focus, these studies indicatively include: Allen (2014) and Allen et al.'s (2013) investigations into street-level violence targeting visible Muslim women; Chakraborti and Zempi's (2012) investigation into veiling; Moosavi's (2012) study of the experience of Islamophobia among white Muslim converts; the opposition shown towards the development of new mosques by Gale (2005) and Landman and Wessels (2005); and the experience of online hate by Awan and Zempi (2016) and Awan and Zempi (2016).

A Joined Up, 'Real' Understanding

Joining up Islamophobia in this way is important, not least in addressing the criticisms of Hargreaves (2015) previously that some scholarly studies conceive Islamophobia as an all-encompassing phenomenon that in turn lacks specificity while others typically adduce broad conclusions about Islamophobia more generally from relatively small sample sizes. It also goes some way to allay Vakil's (2010) concerns about the need for Islamophobia to be more meaningful. In seeking to 'join up' Islamophobia in this way, it also helps bridge Part I of this book with Part II. Underpinning this part has been the contestation attributed to the phenomenon of Islamophobia and how best to define and conceive it as a discriminatory phenomenon. In the following part, Islamophobia is evidenced as a 'real' and tangible phenomenon: one that is neither necessarily political nor academic. Accordingly, any conception and definition of Islamophobia has to be appropriately 'real' as well. As considered in this chapter and preceding chapters, that process is far from straightforward: at least if the deliberating process of definition that is ongoing in the political and public spaces is anything to go by. If Islamophobia is to be reconfigured, as a means of offering something that is a little more 'real', this process is not only extremely urgent but so too desperately needed.

This is where considering Islamophobia as necessarily akin to other ideologically informed discriminatory phenomenon is most crucial and most beneficial. As Allen (2010a) established—and subsequently went on to develop (Allen, 2017)—what is known and understood about Muslims and Islam is embedded in variously complex systems of signifiers and symbols that shape and inform the social consensus. Accordingly, Islamophobia is not restricted to any specific action, practice or discrimination but is evident in a vast array of different social, political and cultural processes whereby the identification and recognition of Muslims and Islam as a problematised 'Other' is accepted and consumed without question or contestation. While that which is subsequently known and understood about Muslims and Islam are little more than mere ideological constructs, what becomes evident is how the ideological aspect of Islamophobia—similarly with racism and other discriminatory phenomena—informs the exclusionary practices and acts of violence referred to previously.

Allen further elaborates on this by citing Clarke (2003). For him, such ideological constructs function through reinforcing and reifying notions that purport to demarcate who 'we' are from who 'we' are not. Through processes of stigmatisation and marginalisation, an unquestioned acceptance ensues, whereby all Muslims and Islam without differentiation become an essentialised homogenous entity. Undeniably 'Other', the certain set of prejudices, opinions and attitudes referred to previously are therefore at once not only irremovable but so too eternally fixed. Referred to as 'normative truths', not only do these inform what Allen (2010a) describes as 'Islamophobia thinking' but so too do they become the primary means through which Muslims and Islam are known and subsequently understood. In this way, the normative truths confer—among others—the view that it is 'common sense' to be suspicious and fearful of Muslims and Islam, thereby becoming the premise upon which it becomes relatively easy to rationalise and justify the need to respond or resist while also hating and deploying acts of violence (Allen, 2017). Consequently, the normative truths provide a means by which those seeking to vent anger, bigotry or hate—whether in the form of violence or not—are able to locate and source justification and legitimacy. Though it is necessary to stress that not all recipients of such normative truths are Islamophobic, 'Islamophobia thinking' is far from the preserve of those who seek to use acts of violence against Muslims.

These latterly referred to acts of violence equate to the 'real' and tangible manifestations of Islamophobia referred to in the introduction: the hate crimes recorded in official data and whose numbers are known to be rapidly rising (O'Neill, 2017). Accordingly, a tangible Islamophobia—largely equivalent to Islamophobic hate crime—can be understood as any malicious or violent act directed at Muslims (or those perceived to be Muslim) or any material entity associated with them (including mosques) where there exists evidence that the motivation, content or perpetrator focused on a perceived Muslim identity or other symbol of Muslims or Islam. Not only is there independently verified evidence that this tangible Islamophobia exists but so too is it possible to conceive a definition that is specific and constrained enough to navigate the tried and tested arguments of the critics and detractors. Derived from scholarly conceptions and definitions, it duly demarcates the tangible from the political. So too does it demarcate those manifestations of Islamophobia that detrimentally affect the lives of ordinary people who happen to be Muslim—or are perceived to be—and the unnecessarily broad conceptions and definitions of Islamophobia that encompass the potentially problematic far more nebulous and complex issues relating to state scrutiny, counter-terror policy and media representation among others. The following chapter sets out how, in the context of this book, this real and tangible Islamophobia was investigated and subsequently evidenced.

References

Allen, C. (2010a). *Islamophobia*. Farnham: Ashgate.

Allen, C. (2010b). Islamophobia: From KISS to RIP. In S. Sayyid & A. Vakil (Eds.), *Thinking through Islamophobia: Global perspectives* (pp. 51–64). London: Hurst & Co.

Allen, C. (2014). Exploring the impact of Islamophobia on visible Muslim women victims: A British case study. *Journal of Muslims in Europe, 3*(2), 137–159.

Allen, C. (2017). Islamophobia and the Problematization of Mosques: A Critical Exploration of Hate Crimes and the Symbolic Function of "Old" and "New" Mosques in the United Kingdom. *Journal of Muslim Minority Affairs, 37*(3), 294–308.

Allen, C., Isakjee, A., & Ögtem-Young, Ö. (2013). *Maybe we are hated: The experience and impact of anti-Muslim hate on British Muslim women*. Birmingham: University of Birmingham.

Awan, I., & Zempi, I. (2016). The affinity between online and offline anti-Muslim hate crime: Dynamics and impacts. *Aggression and Violent Behavior, 27*, 1–8.

BBC News. (2019). US House condemns Trump attacks on congresswomen as racist. *BBC News*. Retrieved from https://www.bbc.co.uk/news/world-us-canada-49011843

Carr, J. (2016). *Experiences of Islamophobia: Living with racism in the neoliberal era*. Abingdon: Routledge.

Chakraborti, N., & Zempi, I. (2012). The veil under attack: Gendered dimensions of Islamophobic victimization. *International Review of Victimology, 18*(3), 269–284.

Clarke, S. (2003). *Social theory, psychoanalysis and racism*. Basingstoke: Palgrave Macmillan.

Gale, R. (2005). Representing the city: Mosques and the planning process in Birmingham. *Journal of Ethnic and Migration Studies, 31*(6), 1161–1179.

Halliday, F. (1999). *Islam and the myth of confrontation: Religion and politics in the Middle East*. London: I.B. Tauris.

Hargreaves, J. (2015). Half a story? Missing perspectives in the criminological accounts of British Muslim communities, crime and the criminal justice system. *British Journal of Criminology, 55*(1), 19–38.

Helbling, M. (2010). Islamophobia in Switzerland: A new phenomenon or a new name for xenophobia? In S. Hug & H. Kriesi (Eds.), *Value change in Switzerland* (pp. 65–80). Lanham: Lexington Books.

Hödl, K. (2010). Islamophobia in Austria: The recent emergence of anti-Muslim sentiments in the country. *Journal of Muslim Minority Affairs, 30*(4), 443–456.

Hussain, D. (2004). The impact of 9/11 on British Muslim identity. In R. Geaves (Ed.), *Islam and the West: A post September 11th perspective* (pp. 115–129). London: Ashgate.

Jackson, L. B. (2018). *Islamophobia in Britain: The making of a Muslim enemy*. Cham: Palgrave Macmillan.
Kayaoglu, A., & Kaya, A. (2012). *A quantitative analysis of Islamophobia in EU-15*. Leuven: University of Leuven.
Klug, B. (2012). Islamophobia: A concept comes of age. *Ethnicities, 12*(5), 665–681.
Kühnel, S., & Leibold, J. (2007). Islamophobie in der deutschen Bevölkerung: ein neues Phänomen oder nur ein neuer Namen? Ergebnisse von Bevölkerungsumfragen zur Gruppenbezogenen Menschenfeindlichkeit 2003 bis 2005. In M. Wohlrab-Sahr & L. Tezcan (Eds.), *Konfliktfeld Islam in Europa* (pp. 135–154). Baden-Baden: Nomos.
Landman, N., & Wessels, W. (2005). The visibility of mosques in Dutch towns. *Journal of Ethnic and Migration Studies, 31*(6), 1125–1140.
Miles, R. (1989). *Racism*. London: Routledge.
Miles, R., & Brown, M. (2003). *Racism*. London: Psychology Press.
Milton-Edwards, B. (2002). Researching the radical: The quest for a new perspective. In H. Donnan (Ed.), *Interpreting Islam* (pp. 32–50). London: Sage.
Moosavi, L. (2012). British Muslim converts performing 'authentic Muslimness'. *Performing Islam, 1*(1), 103–128.
Moosavi, L. (2014). Orientalism at home: Islamophobia in the representations of Islam and Muslims by the New Labour government. *Ethnicities, 14*(3), 1–23.
O'Neill, A. (2017). *Hate crime, England and Wales, 2016/17: Statistical bulletin 17/17*. London: Home Office.
Sardar, Z. (1995). Racism, identity and Muslims in the West. In S. Z. Abedin & Z. Sardar (Eds.), *Muslim minorities in the West* (pp. 1–17). London: Grey Seal.
Sayyid, S. (2010). Thinking through Islamophobia. In S. Sayyid & A. Vakil (Eds.), *Thinking through Islamophobia: Global perspectives* (pp. 1–4). London: Hurst & Co.
Schwarz, T., & Cauchon, S. (2012). *Not in my backyard: 'Nordic' secularism and the rise of Islamophobia*. Annual Meeting of the Western Political Science Assn. March 22–24.
Sheehi, S. (2011). *Islamophobia: The ideological campaign against Muslims*. New York: SCB Distributors.
Shyrock, A. (2010). *Islamophobia Islamophilia: Beyond the politics of enemy and friend*. Bloomington: Indiana University Press.
Taras, R. (2012). *Xenophobia and Islamophobia in Europe*. Edinburgh: Edinburgh University Press.
Tyrer, D. (2013). *The politics of Islamophobia: Race, power and fantasy*. London: Pluto.
Vakil, A. (2010). Who's afraid of Islamophobia? In S. Sayyid & A. Vakil (Eds.), *Thinking trough Islamophobia: Global Perspectives* (pp. 271–279). London: Hurst.
Wieviorka, M. (1995). *The arena of racism*. London: Sage.
Wolfreys, J. (2018). *Republic of Islamophobia: The rise of respectable racism in France*. London: Hurst & Co.
Zemni, S. (2011). The shaping of Islam and Islamophobia in Belgium. *Race & Class, 53*(1), 28–44.

CHAPTER 4

Inside, Outside and Face to Face: Methodological Approaches to Researching Islamophobia

In relation to the existing literature, Hargreaves identifies two extremely pertinent concerns about the scholarly investigation into Islamophobia (Hargreaves, 2015). The first relates to how Islamophobia is routinely conceived as an all-encompassing phenomenon; something one might point to as having potential detrimental ramifications as regards the contestation referred to in previous chapters. Citing insufficient specificity, Hargreaves highlights how some studies aggregate a vast range of different issues—many that go beyond manifestations of discrimination, bigotry and hate—under the broad umbrella of Islamophobia without explanation or evidence. As he rightly notes, many of these are politically resonant and include notions of state scrutiny, counter-terror policies and media representation among various others. To this extent, the line between tangible manifestations of Islamophobia that target individual Muslims and their communities and a vast array of socio-political systems and processes that potentially shape how people think and act towards Muslims is obfuscated. His second centres on scholarly studies that specifically investigate tangible manifestations of Islamophobia. For him, too much emphasis is placed on the overly broad conclusions that are typically adduced from primarily small-scale qualitative studies.

The research undertaken for this book not only took on board these concerns but so too sought to appropriately respond to them, especially when designing a suitably rigorous and robust methodology. Showing significant originality and innovation, this book deploys a methodology that

C. Allen, *Reconfiguring Islamophobia*, Palgrave Hate Studies,
https://doi.org/10.1007/978-3-030-33047-7_4

draws together three distinct approaches to data and evidence gathering. The first comprises a detailed review and analysis of existing literature about Islamophobia. Given this book's remit and focus, this review and analysis not only comprised the growing, albeit still relatively embryonic, scholarly canon but also importantly took in a detailed review of appropriate political and policy-focused resources including appropriate grey literatures. Accordingly, these variously included government reports, third sector and advocacy-focused briefings and documents, policy statements and papers among others. It was also necessary to consider the growing body of non-specialist material about Islamophobia that is available in the media and online spaces. This was particularly necessary in ensuring a comprehensive understanding of the contestation attributed to Islamophobia. The second methodological approach comprised mixed-method qualitative approaches that included in-depth semi-structured interviews and focus groups with male and female victims of tangible, street-level Islamophobic hate crimes as also those able to speak with authority about tangible hate crimes targeting the material entities associated with Muslims and Islam. The third approach comprised the 'insider' experience gained through being an independent adviser that, among others, afforded access to a vast array of previously unpublished documents and similar resources. The latter two approaches are considered in greater detail below.

Engaging Victims of Islamophobia

In researching this book, evidence was gathered from 119 individuals who self-identified as being Muslim, each of whom had—in albeit different ways—experienced a tangible manifestation of Islamophobia in a 'real-world' setting. It is important to note that not all of those engaged chose to identify as victims, hence why the term respondent is preferred throughout. That engagement with respondents comprised three small-scale studies conducted between 2014 and 2017. While each of the small-scale studies were slightly different, each focused on the experience of Islamophobic hate crime and employed topic guides that were consistent as regards both the type and focus of questions asked. To ensure the highest levels of reliability, validity and objectivity, all the gathered data was necessarily critically appraised (Cohen & Crabtree, 2008). This appraisal comprised reviewing the ethical requirements of each of the small-scale studies, investigating matters of consistency and rigour, evaluating differences between methodological approaches and considering the methods through which data was gathered for clarity and consistency (Hannes, 2011). While the critical appraisal did not highlight any problems, a further safeguard put in place to ensure maximum robustness and trustworthiness was to narrow the focus of the data gathered (Cohen & Crabtree, 2008). In this respect, the data analysed and duly analysed here focused solely on the respondent's experience of Islamophobic hate crime (manifestation), what was said and occurred during their experience (content) and how their experience made them—and those around them—feel (impact).

The data for this book was gathered using two well-established qualitative methodological approaches: semi-structured interviews and focus groups. Both approaches involved transcribing verbatim scripts detailing the respondents' answers in their own words and phrases. Duly coding the transcripts, a series of categories of interest were identified from which additional themes, subthemes and patterns were identified. As regards the semi-structured interviews, a total of 60 respondents were engaged. Of those, 20 focused on the female victim experiences of Islamophobic hate crime, 20 on the male experience and 20 on experiences that targeted material entities associated with Muslims and Islam. The latter comprised 14 male respondents and 6 female respondents. As regards the focus groups, a total of 59 individuals participated, of whom 38 were female and 21 male. Across the two data-gathering approaches, 53 per cent respondents were female and 47 per cent male; a slightly disproportionate split that reflects how Muslim women are more likely to experience street-level Islamophobic hate crime than Muslim men (Allen, 2014, 2015; Allen, Isakjee, & Ögtem-Young, 2013; Allen & Nielsen, 2002; Chakraborti & Zempi, 2012). Across the two approaches, the age range of respondents was necessarily broad: from 18 years of age through to 70. While the semi-structured interviews reflected this broad spectrum of ages, it is worth noting that the composition of the focus groups was typically younger; the youngest respondent being 18 and the oldest being 28. While the semi-structured interviews were undertaken in various locations across the country, primarily in urban conurbations, the focus groups were held in the West Midlands and covered the local authority areas of Birmingham, Dudley, Sandwell, Walsall and Wolverhampton.

As is widely acknowledged, Britain's Muslim communities are extremely diverse and comprise a broad number of different ethnicities. While the ethnic make-up of respondents reflected this diversity, because the sampling was necessarily non-probabilistic and purposive—see below—it was not possible to recruit a sample group that was nationally representative. While this raises questions about the generalisability of the findings, it is important to note Polit and Beck's (2010) view that qualitative generalisability is somewhat utopian as also Marshall (1996) and Morse's (1999) observation that generalisability is not the sole measure of important research. Accordingly, 53 respondents identified as being of Pakistani heritage (44 per cent, figures rounded to nearest whole number), 16 Bangladeshi (13 per cent), 14 Somali (12 per cent), 11 Indian (9 per cent), 6 Yemeni (5 per cent), 6 White British (5 per cent), 5 Arab (4 per cent), 3 Black British (3 per cent), 2 Eritrean (2 per cent), 2 Turkish (2 per cent) and 1 Kurdish (less than 1 per cent). It is necessary to stress that in spite of their respective identities—and the content of certain normative truths about Muslims—all identified as British, albeit British with vastly different ethnicities and heritages.

In terms of the recruitment of respondents, the existing scholarly literature highlights a number a number of challenges researchers encounter when trying to engage victims of Islamophobic hate crime (Allen, 2014, 2015, 2017; Zempi & Awan, 2016). One of the most pressing is because up to 70 per cent of all Islamophobic hate crimes are never reported to statutory organisations or services (Fundamental Rights Agency, 2009). As such, it is difficult for researchers to know exactly who has been a victim of Islamophobic hate crime and, importantly, where one might go to recruit them. To overcome this, each of the small-scale studies were co-designed and co-produced with different organisations and groups that worked within Muslim communities to support victims of Islamophobic hate crime. Given that relationships of trust had already been established with those reporting attacks, staff and volunteers within each of the organisations were able to first identify and secondly recruit appropriate respondents for the studies. Acting as a bridgehead, staff and volunteers therefore made initial contact with potential respondents as a means of introducing them to the research undertaken, answering and responding to any initial concerns or questions respondents might have, and if progressing to an appropriate stage, obtain the necessary consent to facilitate an introduction between respondent and researcher.

As before, sampling was therefore necessarily non-probabilistic and purposive given the constraints of identifying those that had experienced Islamophobic hate crimes and were necessarily trusting to participate and share their experience. Again and as before, such an approach has implications for generalisability. While so, the fact that all respondents had direct knowledge and experience of hate crimes being perpetrated against them also meant that their identification and subsequent participation was wholly appropriate. Zempi and Awan (2016) agree, adding that when it comes to researching the experience of Islamophobic hate crime, not only is this an effective approach to sampling, but so too does it ensure you include respondents that are necessarily 'information rich'. As they go on, such approaches are preferable to those that follow a rigid recruitment procedure in that they offer the necessary and desired flexibility to ensure a diverse range of respondents are recruited among whom a wide variety of experiences are manifested. This is readily apparent as regards the gender, age and ethnic variety evident among the respondents upon which the research for this book is founded.

Positionality: Both Insider and Outsider

Potentially the most original and innovative aspect of this book is the methodological approach that draws on the author's unrivalled 'insider' experience gained as an independent adviser on Islamophobia and associated issues to successive British governments, political actors, local governments and various third-sector stakeholders over the past decade and a half. Best described as roles requiring participation on the basis of being an independent 'expert', participation was always necessarily—and rightly—non-partisan and non-remunerated. Nonetheless, the various roles engaged afforded an unprecedented number of opportunities to engage with British Governmental ministers, members of Parliament and numerous other appropriate political actors, including both Muslims and non-Muslims that had been co-opted to represent a range of civil society and community organisations and groups. To understand and explain this 'insider' approach, a twofold characterisation is appropriate. The first relates to the access afforded to previously unpublished documents and resources only made available to those who participated in such roles and the groups associated with them. The second is the engagement that occurred in the form of face-to-face meetings, workshops and both formal and informal conversations, along with electronic communications including emails, online forums and sharing of documents. Throughout this process, extensive research notes were kept that detailed observations, reflections and thoughts as appropriate and which are drawn upon here as a means of shaping and informing thinking while also providing unique and original evidence.

When adopting such an approach, it is necessarily appropriate to reflect on the significance of one's own positionality, to understand the role and function of being a researcher that was both participant and participatory within the political spaces and mechanisms simultaneously being researched. As per Allen (2017), it is likely that while being both participant and participatory, some obfuscation of the boundaries between insider and outsider perspectives would have occurred. While participation and participatory endeavours fall short of Huisman's (2008) activist research, such participation and participatory endeavours did afford unprecedented access to the political spaces, actors and mechanisms that have shaped and informed—to date at least—existing understandings and responses to Islamophobia in the British political spaces. While noting how knowledge about these spaces, actors and mechanisms are as invisible as they are inaccessible to most, Spano's (2005, 2006) oft-cited criticism is that such approaches typically result in one's objectivity being jeopardised. While necessarily acknowledging and, indeed, reflecting on this throughout, one must always counter such criticisms by questioning the extent to which true objectivity is ever realistically achievable. Accordingly, this book—and the research informing it—is of the opinion that the embodied knowledge inherited via such participation and participatory approaches significantly—and unequivocally—outweighs concerns about lack of objectivity (Heidegger, 2002; Sherif, 2001).

When reflecting on the significance of one's own positionality, one must also consider the multiple variables that not only function towards being an 'insider' but so too those that position the researcher as an 'outsider' (Bourke, 2014). Such variables include an array of overlapping social and cultural characteristics that are neither fixed nor limited but which typically include gender, ethnicity, class, religion, sexual orientation, political stance and social standing. Because of the asymmetric nature of one's own multiple identities, that which affords the researcher 'insider' status in one context has the potential to demarcate them as 'outsider' in another. That the self-identities of the researcher may not always be in alignment with the identities attributed or perceived by those being engaged adds further complexity that in turn have the potential to cause both internal and external tensions. As regards the research for this book, being a participant and participatory within the political spaces at times challenged and problematised the author's political views as also the author's self-identification as working class. As regards the latter, the author's cultural and socio-economic background resulted in feelings of being an outsider if not necessarily an imposter (Sherman, 2013). For this reason, it was necessary to engage in an ongoing reflexive process, self-scrutinising one's own role and function as both participant and participatory as a means of maintaining a self-conscious awareness of the potential effect such might have on the evidence and data being gathered (Merriam et al., 2001).

Far from challenging the author in the same way, there was some recognition of the need for self-awareness when engaging male and female Muslim respondents. Through identifying as white, male and British, the author was aware—and indeed has been for the near two decades undertaking this type of research—that these characteristics have the potential to not only construct barriers between researcher and respondent but so too reinforce insider-outsider notions and barriers. Like Milner (2007), experience has shown that when undertaking this type of research, it is less about being from the same racial, ethnic, religious or cultural community as the respondent and more about being actively engaged, thoughtful, trustworthy, authentic and aware of the sensitivities that are important to those being engaged. Through an ongoing process of self-analysis, the author has not only sought to improve and refine these characteristics but so too demonstrate a social and political commitment—as also an authenticity—to the issues being investigated and the communities impacted by them. This has enabled the author to transcend certain boundaries between different communities, most notably those relating to religion and the need to profess one's own religious—or otherwise—leanings. Through being authentic and building trust, these barriers have been minimised.

Political Mechanisms, Policy Interventions

Given the resonance and relevance of the policy spaces to the political equivalent, it is necessary to consider the known limitations of political mechanisms and policy interventions designed to address discriminatory phenomena. For Blakemore and Drake (1996) as also Daniels and Macdonald (2005), it is important to remind ourselves that political mechanisms and policy interventions only typically function to curb certain behaviours: they rarely function to change public opinions, attitudes or thinking. As Bhavani, Mirza, and Meetoo (2005) further elaborate, political mechanisms and interventions are designed to address the effects of discriminatory phenomena, not the causes. For them then, it is necessary to understand that such mechanisms and interventions function at the micro rather than macro level. When applied to the contemporary study of Islamophobia (Allen, 2014), any such political mechanism or policy intervention is rather more likely to go some way to curbing the activities of those perpetrating Islamophobia—criminalising the perpetration of street-level Islamophobic hate crimes for instance—rather than challenge what people commonly 'think' and subsequently 'know' about Muslims and Islam. This is because macro forms of discriminatory phenomena are extremely complex and are likely to be resultant of centuries of asymmetric power relations (Allen, 2010).

In terms of addressing discriminatory phenomena—albeit neither necessarily nor specifically Islamophobia—Afridi (2015) identifies a range of political mechanisms and policy interventions that have been routinely deployed in recent decades. These variously include: legal sanctions and enforcement; education and training; changing procedures within institutions; counselling and mentoring; target setting; increased monitoring; and cross-community interaction. In line with this, Bhavani et al. (2005) offer two definitional categories within which all can be placed: formal and informal. In this way, formal interventions might typically refer to new policies or legislation introduced or put in place. As regards informal interventions, these are typically somewhat more fluid and incorporate less well-defined projects, initiatives and targeted activities. The latter can also include political discourses and narratives. In this book, reference to formal and informal categorisations will be used as and when appropriate, not only as a means of improving understanding but so too positioning the political mechanisms and policy interventions implemented to address Islamophobia within the broader focus of how other similar discriminatory phenomena have been addressed historically.

References

Afridi, A. (2015). *From benign neglect to Citizen Khan: 30 years of equalities practice in Birmingham*. Birmingham: BRAP.

Allen, C. (2010). *Islamophobia*. Farnham: Ashgate.

Allen, C. (2014). Exploring the impact of Islamophobia on visible Muslim women victims: A British case study. *Journal of Muslims in Europe, 3*(2), 137–159.

Allen, C. (2015). 'People hate you because of the way you dress': Understanding the invisible experiences of veiled British Muslim women victims of Islamophobia. *International Review of Victimology, 21*(3), 287–301.

Allen, C. (2017). Islamophobia and the problematization of mosques: A critical exploration of hate crimes and the symbolic function of "old" and "new" mosques in the United Kingdom. *Journal of Muslim Minority Affairs, 37*(3), 294–308.

Allen, C., Isakjee, A., & Ögtem-Young, Ö. (2013). *Maybe we are hated: The experience and impact of anti-Muslim hate on British Muslim women*. Birmingham: University of Birmingham.

Allen, C., & Nielsen, J. S. (2002). *Summary report on Islamophobia in the EU after 11 September 2001*. Vienna: EUMC.

Bhavani, R., Mirza, H. S., & Meetoo, V. (2005). *Tackling the roots of racism: Lessons for success*. Bristol: Policy Press.

Blakemore, K., & Drake, R. F. (1996). *Understanding equal opportunity policies*. New York: Prentice Hall Professional Technical Reference.

Bourke, B. (2014). Positionality: Reflecting on the research process. *The Qualitative Report, 19*(33), 1–9.

Chakraborti, N., & Zempi, I. (2012). The veil under attack: Gendered dimensions of Islamophobic victimization. *International Review of Victimology, 18*(3), 269–284.

Cohen, D. J., & Crabtree, B. F. (2008). Evaluative criteria for qualitative research in health care; Controversies and recommendations. *Annals of Family Medicine, 6*(4), 331–339.

Daniels, K., & Macdonald, L. A. C. (2005). *Equality, diversity and discrimination*. London: Chartered Institute of Personnel and Development.

Fundamental Rights Agency. (2009). *Data in focus report: Muslims*. Vienna: European Union Agency for Fundamental Rights.

Hannes, K. (2011). Critical appraisal of qualitative research. In J. Noyes, A. Booth, K. Hannes, A. Harden, J. Harris, S. Lewin, & C. Lockwood (Eds.), *Supplementary guidance for inclusion of qualitative research in Cochrane systematic reviews of interventions*. Cochrane Collaboration Qualitative Methods Group. Retrieved from http://cqrmg.cochrane.org/supplemental-handbook-guidance

Hargreaves, J. (2015). Half a story? Missing perspectives in the criminological accounts of British Muslim communities, crime and the criminal justice system. *British Journal of Criminology, 55*(1), 19–38.

Heidegger, M. (2002). *On time and being*. Chicago: University of Chicago Press.

Huisman, K. (2008). Does this mean you're not going to come visit me anymore? An inquiry into an ethics of reciprocity and positionality in feminist ethnographic research. *Sociological Inquiry, 78*, 372–396.

Marshall, M. N. (1996). Sampling for qualitative research. *Family Practice, 13*(6), 522–526.

Merriam, S. B., Johnson-Bailey, J., Lee, M. Y., Kee, Y., Ntseane, G., & Muhamad, M. (2001). Power and positionality: Negotiating insider/outsider status within and across cultures. *International Journal of Lifelong Education, 20*(5), 405–416.

Milner IV, H. R. (2007). Race, culture, and researcher positionality: Working through dangers seen, unseen, and unforeseen. *Educational Researcher, 36*(7), 388–400.

Morse, J. M. (1999). Qualitative generalizability. *Qualitative Health Research, 9*(1), 5–6.

Polit, D. F., & Beck, C. T. (2010). Generalization in quantitative and qualitative research: Myths and strategies. *International Journal of Nursing Studies, 47*(11), 1451–1458.

Sherif, B. (2001). The ambiguity of boundaries in the fieldwork experience: Establishing rapport and negotiating insider/outsider status. *Qualitative Inquiry, 7*, 436–447.

Sherman, R. O. (2013). Imposter syndrome: When you feel like you're faking it. *American Nurse Today, 8*(5), 57–58.

Spano, R. (2005). Potential sources of observer bias in police observational data. *Social Science Research, 34*, 591–617.

Spano, R. (2006). Observer behavior as a potential source of reactivity: Describing and quantifying observer effects in a large-scale observational study of police. *Sociological Methods & Research, 34*, 521–553.

Zempi, I., & Awan, I. (2016). *Islamophobia: Lived experiences of online and offline victimisation*. Bristol: Policy Press.

PART II

Real and Tangible Manifestations

CHAPTER 5

From Go Back Home to Letterboxes: Islamophobia and Muslim Women

The number of scholarly studies investigating Muslim women has been growing over the past two decades. Whilst some have been broadly approached (Abu-Lughod, 2002), others have tended to be rather more location specific, for instance, Wing and Smith (2005), Bowen (2007) and Fernando (2009) in France, Jouili and Amir-Moazami (2006) as also Amir-Moazami (2011) in Germany, Salih (2001) in Italy, Bracke (2011) in the Netherlands, Predelli (2004) in Norway, Helbling in Switzerland (2010) and McGinty (2007) in Sweden. Much of this existing literature has focused on the negotiation of Muslim women's identities in the context of the 'Western' world. These include Ali (1992), Knott and Khokher (1993), Afshar (1994), Dwyer (2000), Brown (2002, 2008) and Haw (2010). A primary focus of these studies has been the visibility of Muslim women who wear the hijab or niqab, see, for instance, the studies of Dwyer (2000), Tarlo (2007) and Afshar (2008) among others.

So too has this visibility played out in the public and political spaces, most evident in the raft of legislation introduced in recent years banning the wearing of face veils in a number of different European states. At the time of writing, bans of varying degrees existed in Austria, Belgium, Bulgaria, Denmark, France, Italy and the Netherlands among others. Maybe most telling as regards the problematisation of Muslim women's visibility occurred in 2016 when the French ban on wearing face veils was extended to ban Muslim women from wearing full-body swimwear—popularly known as 'the burkini'—from a number of beaches in the south of

C. Allen, *Reconfiguring Islamophobia*, Palgrave Hate Studies,
https://doi.org/10.1007/978-3-030-33047-7_5

the country including Cannes, Sisco and Villeneuve-Loubet. The decision to do so was taken on the premise that Muslim women wearing burkinis were deemed to pose a threat to public order (Allen, 2016). Accordingly, anyone found wearing such a garment would receive a caution along with a fine of €38. As Thierry Migoule, the head of municipal services in Cannes, put it at the time: 'Beachwear which ostentatiously displays religious affiliation, when France and places of worship are currently the target of terrorist attacks, is liable to create risks of disrupting public order, which it is necessary to prevent' (cited in Allen, 2016). While the notion of fining someone for wearing too much clothing on a beach appears ludicrous, the images that emerged of Muslim women being forcibly removed from beaches evidenced just how publicly and politically problematised Muslim women's visibility had become.

It is maybe somewhat unsurprising that the focus on Muslim women's visibility comprises a significant body of the third wave of scholarly studies investigating the encounter and experience of Islamophobia. Among others, these include studies by Franks (2000), Afshar, Aitken, and Franks (2005), Chakraborti and Zempi (2012), Allen (2014, 2015) and Moosavi (2014). In this respect, Chakraborti and Zempi (2012) are right to note how Muslim women's identities have been reduced to the mere recognition of outward manifestations including the hijab, niqab or other recognisable form of Islamic attire (abaya, jilbab, burqa, etc.). As they go on, it is this recognition of the outward (visible) manifestations that contemporarily symbolise Muslim women's identity that in turn prompt an association with a whole range of constructed notions that are inherently and undeniably 'Other' and which embody all that is perceived to be wrong, problematic and threatening about Islam and Muslims. As Allen (2014) puts it, this visibility can in many ways be understood as the contemporary signifier of all that is perceived to be problematic about Muslims and Islam to the extent that Muslim women become the physical embodiment of this same problematisation. For Klaus and Kassel (2005), Muslim women's visibility thereby goes beyond the mere material and physical, transformed into something that is rather more ideological.

While existing studies have focused on visibility and problematisation, an alternative approach is set out here. As regards the former, Muslim women's visibility needs to be understood within the context of Carr's (2016) markers of Muslimness: the hijab and niqab functioning as visible markers that immediately confer recognition and legitimacy on the wearer being Muslim. As regards the latter, the problematisation of Muslim women's identities needs to be understood in the context of Allen's (2010) normative truths. Inadvertently, Chakraborti and Zempi (2012) offer some justification for preferring this particular interpretation given that Muslim women are contemporarily perceived to be more threatening than Muslim men not least because they cannot be mistaken, denied or concealed. Accordingly, as a normative truth about Muslim women it is conferred legitimacy through a marker—or markers—of Muslimness. In this—and following chapters—the relationship between markers of Muslimness and normative truths as regards the real and tangible manifestations of Islamophobia will be investigated. This and subsequent chapters do not seek to 'prove' Islamophobia not least because the experience and testimonies of respondents are enough to assert its existence. Instead, each seeks to improve understanding about what real and tangible Islamophobia looks like as a means of providing new and informed insights that will provide the necessary foundation to reconfigure Islamophobia as a public and political phenomenon in the later section.

Hijabs, Niqabs and a Terrorist Religion

The majority of Muslim women's experiences of Islamophobia are known to be 'low level', most typically involving verbal abuse (Allen & Nielsen, 2002). From the respondents, the verbal abuse experienced took a variety of forms albeit most of which focused on the respondent's visible identity. For some, this was somewhat one-dimensional for instance, '*fucking Muslim*' or '*fuck off Muslim bitch*'. Common among the verbal abuse was the attribution of being Muslim with also being a 'terrorist': one respondent was called a '*fucking Muslim terrorist*' by a group of people she saw on a regular basis. While the incident made her fearful, she was especially scared for her children who were with her at the time. Other respondents experienced similar incidents including verbal abuse that inferred that if they were not themselves terrorists, then they were at least capable of being one. Clearly among perpetrators, there was a relationship between the recognition of being Muslim (markers of Muslimness) with the understanding that they were terrorists or at least terroristic (normative truth). This was particularly evident in the experience of one respondent who, while travelling on a busy commuter train, spoke about how two men repeatedly referred to her as '*a terrorist*'. Having tried to move seats, the respondent recounted how one of the men '*tapped me on my head, making remarks about my hijab*'. Asking her what she kept under it, he then made a mock announcement to passengers nearby that she had a bomb in her bag.

Similar was also evident in the experience of another respondent. Having heard a man say '*terrorist*' under his breath shortly after having to sit next to her on public transport due to a lack of space, the man went on to claim that the respondent was somehow '*intimidating*' him. Asking why, she said he replied '*because you're Muslim*'. While this might suggest the perpetrator was 'scared' or 'fearful' of the Muslim woman that the opening statement accused the respondent of being a 'terrorist' is maybe rather more telling: the accusation she was 'intimidating' seeming to be rather more an excuse or afterthought than anything else. Thinking through markers of Muslimness and normative truths, Chakraborti and Zempi (2012) suggest that contemporarily at least, there is a widespread perception that Islam is a 'terrorist religion'. Accordingly, the recognition of her Muslimness—identifiable via her hijab—meant that she was perceived to adhere to a 'terrorist religion' even if she happened to not be 'a terrorist' herself. Far from being a fear or phobia, the incident can be explained by how the recognition of the Muslim woman's visibility (her hijab functioning as a marker of Muslimness) triggered an interpretation of the respondent's Muslimness—and all that this entails—in entirely stereotypical ways (normative truth).

Markers of Muslimness in the form of the hijab, niqab or other recognisable attire of Muslim women were prominent in the experience of almost all the female respondents. In fact, it was this that seemed to catalyse the ire of various perpetrators. This was evident in the experience of one respondent who recounted how a man violently tried to pull her hijab from her head during her lunch break from work. A few weeks earlier, the same respondent had a similar experience albeit by a woman. The latter experience took place in a hospital during which the female perpetrator not only grabbed her headscarf but so too shouted '*yuck*' in her face. Another respondent had a similar experience at her local gym, the perpetrators in this instance having been known to her for some time. While the respondent had experienced no previous problems, on this occasion a group of women who attended the same class appeared agitated and angry at her presence. Eventually confronting her, the respondent said that as one of the group members grabbed her hijab, another referred to her as '*Mrs Usama bin Laden*': another told her to '*go back to Afghanistan*'. In both incidents, the recognition of markers of Muslimness was clear. In the latter, so too was a quite different set of normative truths associated with those same markers. In this instance, not only was there evidence of homogenisation but so too was there the clear attribution of Muslims as 'Other': that Muslims do not belong here in the UK.

'We're All Pakis': Religion and 'Race'

While the hijab and niqab clearly function as markers of Muslimness, some of the verbal abuse experienced is racialised: highlighting the recurrent intersection and conflation of 'race' with religion. For some respondents, this functioned to 'double-other': unproblematically co-joining overt racialised terms with similarly overt references to Muslimness. Variously manifested, experiences included respondents derogatorily being referred to as '*nigger Muslim*' or '*Muslim monkey*' among others. The most common experience among respondents however was the co-joining of markers of Muslimness with the racialised term 'Paki'. In some ways, this co-joining was wholly normal and routinely accompanied with an insult or aggressive language. One respondent recalled being told, '*fuck off you dirty Paki Muslim*'. What was interesting was how those who described as 'white' were racialised in much the same way. As one female respondent who described herself as a 'white British convert to Islam' recounted, '*we're all "Pakis" in everyone's eyes...all the same, no difference whatsoever... just White Pakis, Paki this, Paki that*'. While this clearly resonates with the findings from Moosavi's (2014) research into the experience of white British converts it gives some insight into how Islamophobia functions rather more akin to racism than it does a fear or phobia. As Carr (2016) explains, akin to how racism deploys biological, somatic or phenotypical markers to define 'otherness', so examples like these illustrate how Islamophobia concomitantly deploys various markers of difference that include 'race', religion and culture to similar effect. In this way, Muslimness not only wholly 'others'—to the extent that irrespective of difference, all Muslims become one and the same—but so too does Muslimness become wholly incompatible with all that is seen to be 'normal' and 'normative' (Allen, 2010).

In addition to being evident in the preceding experiences, this 'otherness' and incompatibility were evident as a precursor to the more high-level Islamophobia experienced by respondents. One spoke about how she was followed by a woman pushing a child in a pram after dropping her own children at school. Routinely called a '*fucking ugly Muslim*' by her follower, when she reached her house the woman hurried towards her and screamed, '*why are you covering your face...why? Are you that ugly...what are you covering your face for?*' As her attacker tried to pull her niqab from her face, the respondent said her attacker also spat at her. Two nights later, the respondent spoke about how a group of people had begun throwing stones at the windows of her house. The respondent recalled her concern for her children given large amounts of glass was scattered around the house when some of the stones broke through the windows. If the two experiences were connected as the respondent unequivocally believed them to be, one might speculate that the 'otherness' attributed to the respondent's niqab was not only enough to prompt the initial attempts to forcibly remove it but so too prompt a group to attack her home. As Allen and Nielsen (2002) previously noted, the visual identifiers of being Muslim and the religion of Islam (both, markers of Muslimness) can be seen to not only prompt but so too justify Islamophobia far more than any genuine fear or threat might.

Another respondent with a similar experience gave voice to this. Having noticed how a large group of youths had recently begun to congregate near her house, the respondent spoke about how the group soon began abusing her about her niqab every time she walked nearby. As the levels of verbal abuse increased, so too did the atmosphere become increasingly aggressive and threatening. This came to a head on evening when two young men from the group went to her home and physically assaulted both her and her brother. While both received court orders banning them from congregating near her home, the respondent said that she continued to see them congregating with the wider group, many of whom continued to abuse and threaten both her and her family. For her, the sole justification for the verbal abuse and physical assault was that she was recognisable as being Muslim. As she put it, '*these people hate us for no apparent reason, they hate us because of our background and our religion*'. Here the respondent is inadvertently noting both the function of markers of Muslimness and the attribution of normative truths that duly ensue. What is important here is that those experiencing Islamophobia are aware of this albeit articulated in a somewhat more straightforward way. None of the respondents ever spoke about Islamophobia in ways that suggested it was a fear or phobia.

Letterboxes and Bank Robbers: Politicising and Problematising

According to the respondents, the focus on them as Muslim women and associated markers of Muslimness was heightened when Muslims and the religion of Islam were in the headlines or were the subject of public or political debate. One respondent remembered how in the wake of the then Home Secretary, Jack Straw claiming the niqab was a barrier to integration (Straw, 2006), she felt a greater sense of hostility from the general public when going about her day-to-day life. As she explained, '*it's never easy wearing the niqab, you're always going to get stares and comments…but after he said that, I just felt so uncomfortable, it wasn't right anywhere. I swear everyone felt I was against them*'. Other niqab-wearing respondents expressed similar, explaining how some people seemed surprised just because they had entered into a conversation with them. While far from being Islamophobic, one respondent recounted a telling encounter. Wearing the niqab and clothing that covered her full body, the respondent spoke about buying a poppy in the run-up to Remembrance Day. As she approached the stand—manned by two servicemen in uniform and an elderly man wearing medals—she said she could sense the tension as she approached them. Trying to be—as she put it—'*bubbly*', she said she spoke openly to the men before putting some coins in the collection and taking a poppy. Continuing the conversation while pinning the poppy to her clothes, she said '*I have no idea what they thought I was going to do*' she said, '*I guess they never thought a Muslim who looked like me would ever wear a poppy. They clearly didn't know that thousands of Muslims fought in the Second World War*'.

As with Straw's comments previously, there was a similar instance in the wake of comments by the current UK Prime Minister, Boris Johnson in the summer of 2018. Writing for *The Telegraph* newspaper (Johnson, 2018), Johnson was responding to Denmark's 'heavy handed attempt' to ban the niqab. Condemning this type of approach, he added that he would always defend the right of Muslim women—and indeed all women—in Britain to wear whatever they prefer. Having stated that however, he included two apparent 'jokes' about Muslim women who wear a face covering: the 'jokes' mocking them for apparently choosing to look like 'letterboxes' or 'bank robbers'. In the week following Johnson's comments, there was a marked increase in the number of hate crimes recorded, targeting Muslim women wearing the niqab (Dearden, 2018). One of the respondents too had a similar experience. Speaking about how she was shouted at by refuse collectors while walking along the street with her children, she recalled how they shouted '*oi, oi, letterbox alert*' just days after Johnson's 'jokes' had made the headlines. While Johnson was condemned for doing so (Allen, 2018), few drew attention to or highlighted the impact his comments had as regards catalysing the real and tangible Islamophobia experienced by Muslim women. Consequently, those doing the condemning again failed to highlight the very real and tangible nature of Islamophobia. Here again, an opportunity to speak about Islamophobia in more meaningful and tangible ways in the public and political spaces was lost.

'Some People Give You a Look Which May Be Nothing...But'

While much is made of understanding the experience of Islamophobia, so too is understanding the impact it has on those who experience equally important. Like those who experience similar albeit motivated by other discriminatory phenomena, experiencing Islamophobia instils fear in its victims (Allen, Isakjee, & Ögtem-Young, 2013). Among respondents, this fear had a significant impact on their everyday lives and how they went about their normal, day-to-day activities. For one respondent, this resulted in her being too scared to go out. When she did, she added, it was always in '*a secretive way*'. For her, this was necessary as her experience had made her suspicious of everyone. Another respondent said she felt no longer able to go '*walking on my own or [out] in the evenings*'. Another spoke about experiencing Islamophobia had resulted in her parents growing increasingly anxious for her safety and well-being, thereby putting pressure on her to keep in touch and let them know everywhere she went. Having experienced both verbal and physical Islamophobia, the respondent also explained how her parents had pleaded with her to stop wearing the hijab. For them, they no longer wanted her to 'look' Muslim as they believed it made her more susceptible to further abuse and violence.

For some, they found themselves projecting their enhanced sense of fear onto their family and friends. For one respondent, this made her fear for the safety of both her seven-month-old baby and her. As she put it:

> *It made me feel very scared...I was scared to go out on the street or into the area on my own. It made me think continuously that I need some sort of self-defence class so I know how to defend myself and protect my children...you start to think that something is going to happen. It kind of makes you feel like somebody is ready to attack you in the street...it kind of makes you think people hate you because of the way you dress. And then you start linking everything as being anti-Muslim and that may well not be the case. For example, some people give you a look which may be nothing...but*

The '*but*' at the end of her comment is particularly telling. While she was aware that most people were unlikely to want to attack her let alone actually do, her experience placed a very real sense of doubt in her mind to the extent that she not only genuinely feared she would experience Islamophobia again but that almost anyone was capable of being the perpetrator. As much as constructing Muslims as an 'other', it would seem the experience of Islamophobia has the potential to function reciprocally also. This was similar for another respondent who explained her experience of Islamophobia: '*kind of makes you think people hate you because of the way you dress. And then you start linking everything as being anti-Muslim and that may well not be the case*'. While few respondents explicitly acknowledged the issue, the comments of numerous others similarly inferred that experiencing Islamophobia had the potential to make individuals rethink or re-evaluate their respective identities as also their sense of belonging. Accordingly, the experience of Islamophobia would seem to make its victims more aware of their differences, demarcating them not only as Muslim but more so as Muslim 'others'. While so, none of the respondents referred to even the slightest inclination that their experience of Islamophobia had made them want to change their Muslim identity.

Given the emphasis placed on Muslim women's visibility and associated identities in the existing scholarly literature, in the context of Islamophobia those same visibilities and identities can be seen to afford a means of identification and recognition that in turn prompts a whole series of meanings and characterisations that shape and inform how Muslims are known and understood. It would therefore seem that both markers of Muslimness as also normative truths are causal in the experience of real and tangible manifestations of Islamophobia. This process—it can be argue—not only allows perpetrators to recognise and identify their victims but so too rationalises and subsequently justifies their actions (Allen, 2015). By investigating real and tangible manifestations of Islamophobia therefore, the experience of Muslim women victims posits Islamophobia as being far more akin to a discriminatory phenomenon than it is a fear or phobia. In truth, there is no evidence whatsoever to suggest that these real experiences of Islamophobia are in any way phobic. While notions of 'race' were an observable element of some of the experiences of Islamophobia—largely as regards the process of 'double-othering'—there was little evidence to suggest that Muslims were seen as a 'race'. Racialised definitely—evident in how the female respondents were undifferentiated, reduced, essentialised and homogenised—markers of Muslimness function akin to how biological or somatic markers do for traditional racism.

In this way, there exists a clear and distinct resonance between how Muslim women are perceived and understood in the public and political spaces and how they are perceived and understood in relation to the experience of real and tangible Islamophobia. While the condemnation following Johnson's comments failed to highlight let alone establish any link between the public and the political and the real and the tangible, it is clear from Muslim women who have experienced Islamophobia that this is indeed the case. As considered in the earlier chapters—and indeed, will be developed later—this would seem to be both endemic and problematic. In the following two chapters, this link is considered in more detail and—importantly—is further evidenced.

References

Abu-Lughod, L. (2002). Do Muslim women really need saving? Anthropological reflections on cultural relativism and its others. *American Anthropologist, 104*(3), 783–790.

Afshar, H. (1994). *Muslim women in West Yorkshire*. London: Taylor and Francis.

Afshar, H. (2008). Can I see your hair? Choice, agency and attitudes: The dilemma of faith and feminism for Muslim women who cover. *Ethnic and Racial Studies, 31*(2), 411–427.

Afshar, H., Aitken, R., & Franks, M. (2005). Feminisms, Islamophobia and identities. *Political Studies, 53*(2), 262–283.

Ali, Y. (1992). Muslim women and the politics of ethnicity and culture in Northern England. In S. Gita & N. Yuval-Davis (Eds.), *Refusing holy orders: Women and fundamentalism in Britain* (pp. 101–123). London: Sage.

Allen, C. (2010). *Islamophobia*. Farnham: Ashgate.

Allen, C. (2014). Exploring the impact of Islamophobia on visible Muslim women victims: A British case study. *Journal of Muslims in Europe, 3*(2), 137–159.

Allen, C. (2015). 'People hate you because of the way you dress': Understanding the invisible experiences of veiled British Muslim women victims of Islamophobia. *International Review of Victimology, 21*(3), 287–301.

Allen, C. (2016). By banning the burkini, the French are blaming Muslims. *HuffPost*. Retrieved from https://www.huffingtonpost.co.uk/dr-chris-allen/burkini-ban-france_b_11535276.html

Allen, C. (2018). It was always Islamophobia, never a 'gaffe': How attention is now being deflected away from Johnson. *Medium*. Retrieved from https://medium.com/@mail.chrisallen/it-was-always-islamophobia-never-a-gaffe-how-attention-is-now-being-deflected-away-from-johnson-c2f1ffc7d8d6

Allen, C., Isakjee, A., & Ögtem-Young, Ö. (2013). *Maybe we are hated: The experience and impact of anti-Muslim hate on British Muslim women*. Birmingham: University of Birmingham.

Allen, C., & Nielsen, J. S. (2002). *Summary report on Islamophobia in the EU after 11 September 2001*. Vienna: EUMC.

Amir-Moazami, S. (2011). Dialogue as a Governmental technique: Managing gendered Islam in Germany. *Feminist Review, 98*(1), 9–27.

Bowen, J. R. (2007). Why the French don't like headscarves: Islam, the state, and public space. *European Review, 15*(3), 397–400.

Bracke, S. (2011). Subjects of debate: Secular and sexual exceptionalism, and Muslim women in the Netherlands. *Feminist Review, 98*(1), 28–46.

Brown, K. (2002). Realising Muslim women's rights: The role of Islamic identity among British Muslim women. *Women's Studies International Forum, 29*(4), 417–430.

Brown, K. (2008). The promise and perils of women's participation in UK mosques: The impact of securitisation agendas on identity, gender and community. *British Journal Politics and International Relations, 10*(3), 472–491.

Carr, J. (2016). *Experiences of Islamophobia: Living with racism in the neoliberal era*. Abingdon: Routledge.

Chakraborti, N., & Zempi, I. (2012). The veil under attack: Gendered dimensions of Islamophobic victimization. *International Review of Victimology, 18*(3), 269–284.

Dearden, L. (2018). 'Letterbox' insults against Muslim women spike in wake of Boris Johnson comments. *The Independent*. Retrieved from https://www.independent.co.uk/news/uk/home-news/boris-johnson-burqa-muslim-women-veil-attacks-islamophobia-letterboxes-rise-a8488651.html

Dwyer, C. (2000). Negotiating diasporic identities: Young British south Asian Muslim women. *Women's Studies International Forum, 23*(4), 475–486.

Fernando, M. (2009). Exceptional citizens: Secular Muslim women and the politics of difference in France. *Social Anthropology, 17*(4), 379–392.

Franks, M. (2000). Crossing the borders of whiteness? White Muslim women who wear the hijab in Britain today. *Ethnic and Racial Studies, 23*(5), 917–929.

Haw, K. (2010). Being, becoming and belonging: Young Muslim women in contemporary Britain. *Journal of Intercultural Studies, 31*(4), 345–361.

Helbling, M. (2010). Islamophobia in Switzerland: A new phenomenon or a new name for xenophobia? In S. Hug & H. Kriesi (Eds.), *Value change in Switzerland* (pp. 65–80). Lanham: Lexington Books.

Johnson, B. (2018). Denmark has got it wrong. Yes, the burka is oppressive and ridiculous – But that's still no reason to ban it. *Telegraph*. Retrieved from https://www.telegraph.co.uk/news/2018/08/05/denmark-has-got-wrong-yes-burka-oppressive-ridiculous-still/

Jouili, J. S., & Amir-Moazami, S. (2006). Knowledge, empowerment and religious authority among pious Muslim women in France and Germany. *The Muslim World, 96*(4), 617–642.

Klaus, E., & Kassel, S. (2005). The veil as a means of legitimisation: An analysis of the interconnectedness of gender, media and war. *Journalism, 6*(3), 335–355.

Knott, K., & Khokher, S. (1993). Religious and ethnic identity among young Muslim women in Bradford. *Journal of Ethnic and Migration Studies, 19*(4), 593–610.

McGinty, A. M. (2007). Formation of alternative femininities through Islam: Feminist approaches among Muslim converts in Sweden. *Women's Studies International Forum, 30*(6), 474–485.

Moosavi, L. (2014). The racialization of Muslim converts in Britain and their experiences of Islamophobia. *Critical Sociology, 41*(1), 41–56.

Predelli, L. N. (2004). Interpreting gender in Islam: A case study of immigrant Muslim women in Oslo, Norway. *Gender & Society, 18*(4), 473–493.

Salih, R. (2001). Confronting modernities Muslim women in Italy. *ISIM Newsletter, 7*, 2.

Straw, J. (2006). I felt uneasy talking to someone I couldn't see. *Guardian*. Retrieved from https://www.theguardian.com/commentisfree/2006/oct/06/politics.uk

Tarlo, E. (2007). Hijab in London: Metamorphosis, resonance and effects. *Journal of Material Culture, 12*(2), 131–156.

Wing, A. K., & Smith, M. N. (2005). Critical race feminism lifts the veil: Muslim women, France, and the headscarf ban. *UC Davis School of Law – Law Review, 39*, 743.

CHAPTER 6

From bin Laden to Paedos: Islamophobia and Muslim Men

As regards Muslim men, the number of scholarly studies relating to their experience is not only far less in number than those focusing on Muslim women but so too has a quite different focus with most typically themed around masculinity. An indicative sample of these might include the studies of Archer (2001), Hopkins (2006), Kalra (2009) and Dagistanli and Grewal (2012) among others. Focusing on factors that are both religious and cultural, these studies comprise a broad interpretation of masculinity albeit typically problematising Muslim men through the various attributions of violence or aggression. Aslam (2012) for instance does this through an exploration of the perceived nexus between Muslim masculinities, jihadist Islamism and terrorism. Given the normative truths of Islamophobia, it may be somewhat unsurprising that matters relating to violence and aggression—as also jihadism and terrorism—are recurrent features in the scholarly canon. Potentially problematic, there is however a similarity between the current literature relating to Muslim men and women, that is, that both evidence an overriding emphasis and focus on that which shapes and informs Islamophobia thinking (Allen, 2010). While so, the approaches deployed through which male Muslim aggression and violence is considered are multifarious. These include approaches that consider patriarchal violence within Muslim migrant communities (Razack, 2004), the specific patriarchal violence and control exerted by Pakistani-heritage men over Pakistani-heritage women (Macey, 1999), the role and perpetration of violence linked to notions of honour (Ewing,

C. Allen, *Reconfiguring Islamophobia*, Palgrave Hate Studies,
https://doi.org/10.1007/978-3-030-33047-7_6

2008) and maybe unsurprisingly, political and terroristic violence as per Hopkins (2007), Macey (2007), and Dwyer, Shah, and Sanghera (2008) among variety of others.

As per Islamophobia and Islamophobic hate crime more specifically, Muslim men are largely non-existent in the third wave of scholarly studies referred to previously. As a result, knowledge about how Islamophobia is experienced by Muslim men is extremely limited. What is known however is best approached using a twofold categorisation. First, what literature does exist suggests that Muslim men are less likely to experience Islamophobia than Muslim women (Allen & Nielsen, 2002). While so, there is little scholarly evidence to support this: that which is known being largely adduced from studies investigating the experience of Islamophobia among Muslim women. Second, and similar to Muslim women, markers of Muslimness appear important despite Muslim men being typically far less recognisable and identifiable than Muslim women. As regards visible identifiers that enable the recognition and identification of Muslim men, a handful of sources do refer to beards (Carr, 2016) and certain forms of Islamic attire (Allen, 2015; Allen & Nielsen, 2002) functioning in this way. In the immediate aftermath of the 9/11 attacks in the United States, reference was also made to men wearing turbans given the media image of Usama bin Laden wearing the same. While a more typical identifier for Sikh men, it is interesting to note the growing incidence of Sikh men experiencing Islamophobia (Awan, 2017; Sian, 2017) including the murder of a Sikh man having been identified as 'Muslim' during a revenge attack for 9/11 (Allen & Nielsen, 2002). As before however, the evidence base is extremely limited.

'Fuck Off Back to Iraq': Geopolitics and Double-Othering

As with Muslim women, the experience of Islamophobic hate crime among male respondents was also primarily 'low level': manifested as verbal abuse, spitting, harassment and mild intimidation. In line with the existing literature as also the evidence in the previous chapter, verbal abuse was primary (Allen, 2014, 2015; Allen & Nielsen, 2002; Zempi & Awan, 2016). As regards Muslim men, the conferring of otherness and, by consequence, a perceived lack of belonging was extremely common. As one respondent recalled:

> *I was on my lunch when this man—he looked in his 40s—just walked past me and old me to fuck off back to Iraq if you don't like it here you dirty fucking Muslim…I didn't know what to do and by the time I did, he'd walked off anyway. Thing is, I've never been out the country and my family are originally from India, nowhere near Iraq.*

Pertinent in the experience of Muslim men was the lack of accuracy as regards the content of the verbal abuse. Maybe unsurprising, the underlying cause of this seemed to focus on the inability of perpetrators to comprehend that neither Muslims nor the religion of Islam formed a part of who they perceived 'us' to be. While some studies have investigated the problematic attribution of otherness—in particular the somewhat more conceptual 'Islam-West' dichotomy (Fuller, 2018; Sayyid, 1997)—a clear 'us' and 'them' was readily apparent in the content of verbal abuse experienced.

The reference to 'Iraq' was also part of a much wider process to have emerged from the male respondents' experience. Across the different experiences, those delivering the verbal abuse regularly and routinely incorporated similar references to other Muslim-majority countries where the UK and United States had been militarily engaged. What was interesting from the experience of Muslim men was the fluid and changing nature of the content of the verbal abuse directed at them. As some respondents explained, the countries they were told to 'go home' to had moved over time and importantly, in line with military conflict. Accordingly, while this type of verbal abuse once focused on Afghanistan and Iraq, more recently male respondents spoke about being told to 'go home' or 'go back' to Syria. Some also spoke about verbal abuse telling them to go and join Islamic State: '*fuck off back to ISIS*'. As with how the normative truths go some way to essentialising and homogenising all Muslims without differentiation, here it would seem to be empirical evidence to support how these translate into ordinary and everyday thinking—Islamophobia thinking—about Muslims and the religion of Islam. In doing so, the experience of male victims of Islamophobic hate crime would seem to suggest a link between the incidence of Islamophobia and incidents and occurrences in the political spaces, in particular geopolitics and 'Western' military conflict.

In line with the experience of Muslim women and the process of 'double-othering', where notions and terminologies of 'race' and religion were evident in the content of verbal abuse, the same was true of Muslim men also. As with their female equivalent, Muslim men experienced verbal abuse that routinely—and unproblematically—co-joined racialised terms and attributions with those about Muslims and Islam. As with Muslim women, some were largely similar including being called '*Muslim nigger*'. Other respondents recalled how their experience had included references to them as '*sand niggers*'. As before however, the most common experience included the co-joining of markers of Muslimness with racialised references being made to 'Paki'. Akin to the experience of Muslim women, male respondents regularly and routinely experienced similar instances, albeit accompanied by a vast array of insults and aggressive additions. One respondent spoke about how a perpetrator shouted '*fuck off you dirty Paki Muslim*' at him, 'dirty' being quite common in the verbal abuse experienced by the male respondents.

'Soldier Killers': The Influence and Impact of Terror Incidents

In line with the following chapter, a number of male respondents reflected on the catalytic influence terror-related incidents seemed to have on the perpetration of Islamophobic hate crimes targeting them. While this seems to suggest that a terror-related incident can be deployed to explain or rationalise an Islamophobic incident—in some ways, as 'revenge'—the experience of male respondents went beyond this, suggesting that those same terror-related incidents also have the potential to shape and inform content. The most obvious and common example of this was the prevalence of Muslim men being called 'terrorist'. While this was also evident in the experience of Muslim women, what was interesting in the experience of male respondents was the preponderance of the association and subsequent attribution of terrorism with violence. As before however, this was far from a static process with attributions and associations changing in line with the changing nature of terrorist incidents. For those that had experienced Islamophobia on multiple occasions over a period of time—common among the respondents engaged—so the content of verbal abuse changed. For those that had experienced Islamophobia a decade or so ago, verbal abuse routinely incorporated reference being made to 9/11 and Al-Qaeda. Similar to the experience of one female respondent earlier, some male respondents that had beards said that they—at various times—had been called '*bin Laden*' and '*Usama*'.

Among those that had experienced Islamophobia over time, there was a general consensus that the murder of Lee Rigby—the British soldier brutally murdered in the street in London in 2013—not only increased the levels of hate directed towards them but so too catalysed a change in the content of verbal abuse experienced. With references to 9/11 confined to the past, two male respondents, respectively, spoke about abuse that accused them of being a '*murderer*' and '*soldier killer*'. The link between terror incidents and hate crime was not lost on them with one adding:

> *[It was] definitely a reaction to recent events…because it [Rigby's murder] was so horrific…the Muslims who do it cause a backlash and antagonise a lot of people…ordinary people like us then get it in the neck…we get the brunt of their, erm, rubbish even though we've done nothing wrong.*

The attribution of 'otherness' is therefore not only acknowledged by the respondents but so too understood to be causal and catalytic.

Shaping and influencing the experience of younger respondents was the emergence of Islamic State and the Civil War more recently in Syria. For some, this was overpowering given the prevalence and routine nature of occurrence in the content of verbal abuse. As one young male respondent explained, he first encountered this while playing football. Playing on a Sunday morning in an amateur league, he said that he noticed how a player on the opposing team mumbled something every time he got near to him. At first, he ignored it, dismissing it as '*one of those things*' typical of amateur football. It was only after he realised the opposing player was saying '*ISIS*' did it begin to make him angry and feel necessitated to react. Talking about how he confronted the player during a stoppage in the game, he said the opposing players reply was '*ISIS cunt*'. As he went on:

> *OK, so I reacted badly, like…I got in his face and everything but he was all like to his mates—this is what they're like, ISIS cunts man. He then looks at me and goes, nah you're not worth it bruv before using his hands to gesture a bomb dropping and exploding.*

Somewhat similarly, another young respondent spoke about how a group of older seemingly drunk men chanted '*ISIS, ISIS, ISIS*' at him as he walked past a beer garden attached to a public house with his sister who was wearing the niqab at the time.

'Muslim Paedo': From 'Grooming Gangs' to the Radical Right

Aside from terror-related incidents, the experience of male victims of Islamophobic hate crime also evidenced the influence and impact of non-terror-related incidents. This was most evident in the widespread use of the term '*paedo*' or '*paedo Muslim*': 'paedo' an abbreviated or colloquial term for paedophile. From speaking with the respondents, those that were older spoke about how rapid and prevalent the use of 'paedo' had become. Among them, there was a consensus view that this was the most common insult nowadays directed at Muslim men. In trying to explain the growth and spread of this particular insult, some respondents noted a correlation with the increased focus in the public and political spaces on a number of high-profile sexual exploitation scandals, many involving men of Pakistani heritage (Tufail & Poynting, 2016). Having looked back to the time when respondents claim the insult first emerged, it would seem that not only does this coincide with an increased coverage of such scandals in the media but so too when the term 'grooming gangs' begun to be more widely used to refer to those perpetrating the crimes. As one male respondent put it, '*people think we're all the same…that's what the media and politicians want, we're all the same to them too*'.

From retrospectively analysing the use of the term during experiences of verbal abuse, there would also seem to be some correlation between usage of the terms 'paedo' and 'grooming gangs' by those in the radical right milieu in particular, when mobilising and organising its supporters to protest against the scandals. In some ways, this is unsurprising given the extent to which the existing literature evidences links between Islamophobia and the adoption of certain socio-political issues by the radical right (Allen, 2010; Gündüz, 2010). It is also useful to note how some of the respondents spoke about the phrase '*paedo religion*' being deployed. While respondents themselves did not make the link, one might posit that there is indeed a link between the content of Islamophobia hate crime and the role and function of the radical right. Similarly, this also goes some way to highlight how history provides a seedbed for contemporary Islamophobia (Allen, 2010; Halliday, 1999), a point made previously. To illustrate this, some radical right actors and groups have drawn attention to how Ayesha was only nine years old when she married the Prophet Muhammad (Tufail, 2015). Translated into the contemporary setting by the British National Party in a way that described 'our girls' being treated like 'halal meat'

(Allen, 2014), they—like numerous others in the radical right—utilised this to explain and subsequently justify the inference that all Muslim men without differentiation are not only open to sexual exploitation but so too paedophilia.

As regards the radical right and history, a number of other tropes emerge from the collective experience of male respondents. Aside from the Ayesha narrative, another feature of the content of the verbal abuse experienced drew on historical perceptions about the religion of Islam to infer is to be an '*evil*' religion. Across the studies, some respondents spoke about verbal abuse associating Islam—and Muslims—with '*the devil*' and '*Satan*'. While none of the respondents made any such link themselves, one cannot dismiss how historically Islam has been routinely decried across Europe as being Satanic whereby Muhammad was understood to be the Antichrist (Allen, 2017; Daniel, 2000; Esposito, 1994). While contemporary experiences of Islamophobia might necessarily require us to focus on the contemporary spaces only, not least because of the catalytic impact evident in relation to both terror- and non-terror-related incidents, it would be inappropriate to dismiss out of hand the role of history. This is not because history is a continuum or that Islamophobia can be retrospectively applied but because it provides a seedbed of ideas, notions and understandings that can be drawn on and subsequently deployed to shape and inform as also rationalise and justify the present day. In doing so, history can be used to rationalise and justify today's normative truths.

'I'd Only Be More Visible if I Started Waving a Flag': The Visibility of Muslim Women

Unlike Muslim women, existing literature relating to the visibility of Muslim men and the function it performs is non-existent. A somewhat straightforward and pragmatic explanation for this might be because most Muslim men—as is likely the case in most 'Western' countries—are typically far less visible than their female equivalent. Nonetheless, some respondents had experienced Islamophobia that seemed to focus on their visibility and how they looked: citing beards, caps and certain types of attire. For the majority of male respondents however, their visibility seemed insignificant and inconsequential. For those for whom it was, however, there were some notable discrepancies and differences from visible Muslim women. While Muslim women respondents spoke about being 'easy targets', it was not always clear what the markers of Muslimness were as regards men. Having been hit across the back of the head and verbally abused by his perpetrator, one respondent reflected on how:

> *he [the perpetrator] must have seen me leave the masjid…how else would he have known I was Muslim? I mean, he did because when he hit me, he called me a 'fucking Muslim' then a 'fucking paedo'…I don't even look like one, do I?*

It is interesting the extent to which the different types of verbal abuse came together in this one experience.

Maybe more interesting is how, like other male respondents, there was a clear acknowledgement among the men engaged about how their visibility had the potential to earmark them as being Muslim and therefore targets for Islamophobia. Among those who were not visibly recognisable as Muslim—void of any obvious markers of Muslimness—a good number questioned how and why they had been duly targeted. As regards those who were visibly recognisable as Muslim, they readily laid claim to their beard, cap or clothing. The previously noted respondent called '*bin Laden*' explained this on the basis that at the time of the experience, he had a large beard and wore turban-type headwear. As he went on, '*to be honest, I could have been Sikh, they wouldn't have known*'. While most of the respondents had not experienced Islamophobia that focused on their visible identity, many said that they were aware of those that had. For some, there was a belief that the more 'Muslim' you looked, the more likely you were to be a victim of Islamophobia. Some expressed real concern about older members of their families who respondents claimed were more likely to wear what they routinely referred to as 'traditional' clothing.

In the same way, some of the female respondents had given thought to changing their appearance—to look 'less' Muslim—so too had some of the male respondents. While—like their female counterparts—none of the male respondents did actually do so, some spoke about how they had changed certain behaviours. Some distance from the more obvious markers of Muslimness associated with Muslim women, one might argue that the behaviours changed were inadvertently informed by the tacit recognition that certain behaviours had the potential to serve as markers of Muslimness that in turn had the potential to link them with certain normative truths. These included carrying rucksacks, reading Arabic texts on phones and tablets and speaking non-English languages all of which were identified by respondents as being particularly problematic on public transport and in public places. In support of the argument that these behaviours have the potential to serve as markers of Muslimness, when asked why they had chosen to change certain behaviours, one male respondent unequivocally stated that it was because he had given serious thought to how he '*might look less Muslim…after all the terror attacks this year [2017]*'. Despite there being no evidence to suggest that these items and behaviours helped recognise and subsequently identify male respondents, it is interesting that those experiencing Islamophobia are—maybe subconsciously—interpreting them as markers of Muslimness. Functioning symbolically—like the hijab and niqab or the physical structures associated with Muslims and Islam—a clear resonance would seem to exist across all the different manifestations of real and tangible Islamophobia investigated and evidenced here.

The Islamophobic Experience of Muslim Men: Same but Different

Noting the concerns of Hargreaves (2015) previously, it would be inappropriate to adduce from this single study any broad conclusions despite the fact it is one of the few studies to investigate the Islamophobic experience of male victims. Nonetheless, some interesting findings do emerge, each of which is likely to require further investigation. The first of these relates to the similarities in evidence as regards the experience of Muslim men and women. In this way, as well as the majority of experiences being low level and involving verbal abuse, there were also distinct similarities in content too not least the co-joining of insults and terminology relating to 'race' and religion that in turn, 'double-other'. As with the female experience, the co-joining of 'Paki' with other more Muslim-specific terms was most common, thereby—and similarly—ensuring that Muslim men be as equally essentialised, homogenised and perceived as being one and the same without differentiation. That these experiences were so similar irrespective of the gender of the victims would suggest that such experiences are not only common but so too indicative of the type of Islamophobia experience others are likely to encounter in their everyday lives.

While so, the experience of Muslim men highlighted a number of stark differences too. This was most notable in how the content of verbal abuse was rather more protean as regards male victims and was seemingly shaped and influenced by both terror-related and non-terror-related incidents and events. As regards the former, what was interesting—and wholly new—was how geopolitics and Western-led military action in Muslim-majority countries appeared to shape and inform that change. While it would be wrong to make unreasonable claims on the back of this, it does highlight the resonance between real and tangible Islamophobia and the discourses and actions that take place in the public and political spaces: a further dimension to the Straw and Johnson discursive link made in the previous chapter. While it might have been thought that terror-related incidents had a catalytic impact on manifestation of Islamophobia, here the evidence seemed to suggest the same was true of certain non-terror-related incidents too. Illustrated by the emergence and development of the term 'paedo', the experience of male respondents afforded another illustration of how the content of verbal abuse changed and transitioned to the extent that many believed that this was now the most common slur directed towards them.

Maybe most interesting was how Muslim men, many of whom are less visible—and thereby less recognisable and identifiable—than many Muslim women, were still identifiable via markers of Muslimness. While these were evident in the wearing of certain types of attire or hats and among those who had beards, what emerged from the experience of some of the male respondents was how certain accessories and activities seemed to function akin to more obvious markers including the hijab and niqab. While the male respondents did not explicitly convey or specifically articulate this, it was clear that their own self-awareness of engaging in certain activities or behaviours was in themselves markers through which they might be recognised and identified and thereby subsequently targeted for Islamophobia. Accordingly, a bearded man carrying a black rucksack not only has the potential to perform the same function as more obvious markers of Muslimness but so too the potential to attribute normative truths also. In line with existing scholarly thinking, it is clear that real and tangible manifestations of Islamophobia are much more akin to manifestations of racism—and indeed other discriminatory phenomena—than they are a fear or phobia.

References

Allen, C. (2010). *Islamophobia*. Farnham: Ashgate.

Allen, C. (2014). Exploring the impact of Islamophobia on visible Muslim women victims: A British case study. *Journal of Muslims in Europe, 3*(2), 137–159.

Allen, C. (2015). 'People hate you because of the way you dress': Understanding the invisible experiences of veiled British Muslim women victims of Islamophobia. *International Review of Victimology, 21*(3), 287–301.
Allen, C. (2017). Islamophobia. In D. Thomas (Ed.), *The Routledge handbook on Christian-Muslim relations* (pp. 376–383). London: Routledge.
Allen, C., & Nielsen, J. S. (2002). *Summary report on Islamophobia in the EU after 11 September 2001*. Vienna: EUMC.
Archer, L. (2001). 'Muslim brothers, black lads, traditional Asians': British Muslim young men's constructions of race, religion and masculinity. *Feminism & Psychology, 11*(1), 79–105.
Aslam, M. (2012). *Gender-based explosions: The nexus between Muslim masculinities, jihadist Islamism and terrorism*. UNU Press.
Awan, I. (2017). The non-Muslims experiencing Islamophobic attacks. *New Statesman*. Retrieved from https://www.newstatesman.com/politics/staggers/2017/10/non-muslims-experiencing-islamophobic-attacks
Carr, J. (2016). *Experiences of Islamophobia: Living with racism in the neoliberal era*. Abingdon: Routledge.
Dagistanli, S., & Grewal, K. (2012). Perverse Muslim masculinities in contemporary orientalist discourse: The vagaries of Muslim immigration in the West. In *Global Islamophobia: Muslims and moral panic in the West* (pp. 119–142). Surrey: Ashgate Publishing Ltd.
Daniel, N. (2000). *Islam and the West: The making of an image*. Oxford: Oneworld.
Dwyer, C., Shah, B., & Sanghera, G. (2008). 'From cricket lover to terror suspect' – Challenging representations of young British Muslim men. *Gender, Place & Culture, 15*(2), 117–136.
Esposito, J. (1994). *The Islamic threat: Myth or reality?* Oxford: Oxford University Press.
Ewing, K. P. (2008). *Stolen honor: Stigmatizing Muslim men in Berlin*. Stanford University Press.
Fuller, G. (2018). *A sense of siege: The geopolitics of Islam and the West*. London: Routledge.
Gündüz, Z. Y. (2010). The European Union at 50—Xenophobia, Islamophobia and the rise of the radical right. *Journal of Muslim Minority Affairs, 30*(1), 35–47.
Halliday, F. (1999). *Islam and the myth of confrontation: Religion and politics in the Middle East*. London: I.B. Tauris.
Hargreaves, J. (2015). Half a story? Missing perspectives in the criminological accounts of British Muslim communities, crime and the criminal justice system. *British Journal of Criminology, 55*(1), 19–38.
Hopkins, P. (2007). Global events, national politics, local lives: Young Muslim men in Scotland. *Environment and Planning A, 39*(5), 1119–1133.

Hopkins, P. E. (2006). Youthful Muslim masculinities: Gender and generational relations. *Transactions of the Institute of British Geographers, 31*(3), 337–352.

Kalra, V. S. (2009). Between emasculation and hypermasculinity: Theorizing British South Asian masculinities. *South Asian Popular Culture, 7*(2), 113–125.

Macey, M. (1999). Religion, male violence, and the control of women: Pakistani Muslim men in Bradford, UK. *Gender & Development, 7*(1), 48–55.

Macey, M. (2007). *Islamic political radicalism in Britain: Muslim men in Bradford*. In T. Abbas (Ed.), *Islamic political radicalism: A European comparative perspective* (pp. 160–172). Edinburgh: Edinburgh University Press.

Razack, S. H. (2004). Imperilled Muslim women, dangerous Muslim men and civilised Europeans: Legal and social responses to forced marriages. *Feminist Legal Studies, 12*(2), 129–174.

Sayyid, S. (1997). *A fundamental fear: Eurocentrism and the emergence of Islamism*. London: Zed Books.

Sian, K. P. (2017). Surveillance, Islamophobia, and Sikh bodies in the war on terror. *Islamophobia Studies Journal, 4*(1), 37–52.

Tufail, W. (2015). Rotherham, Rochdale, and the racialised threat of the 'Muslim Grooming Gang'. *International Journal for Crime, Justice and Social Democracy, 4*(3), 30–43.

Tufail, W., & Poynting, S. (2016). Muslim and dangerous: 'Grooming' and the politics of racialisation. In D. Pratt & R. Woodlock (Eds.), *Fear of Muslims?* (pp. 79–92). Cham: Springer.

Zempi, I., & Awan, I. (2016). *Islamophobia: Lived experiences of online and offline victimisation*. Bristol: Policy Press.

CHAPTER 7

From Smashed Windows to Nail Bombs: Islamophobia and Physical Structures

When considering the physical structures associated with Muslims and the religion of Islam, the existing literature is once again somewhat limited. Where a literature is apparent, the primary focus is mosques with a less prominent and much smaller canon focusing on Islamic schools. As regards the former, that focus is typically framed around considerations of the history and development of Islam or Muslim communities in specific geographical locations. Among others, these include Scriver's (2004) history of mosques in Australia and Jaschok and Shui's (2013) study into women-only mosques in China. As regards the latter, Rashid and Muhammad's (1992) study centres on the Islamic schools in the United States, while Driessen and Merry (2006) adopt a similar frame of inquiry in the Netherlands. Preferring a more comparative approach, Dwyer and Meyer's (1995) study focuses on the development of Islamic education in the UK and Netherlands.

Mosques and Minarets: Problematising Muslims and Islam

As with tangible manifestations of Islamophobia experienced by Muslim men, existing literature investigating Islamophobia targeting physical structures is also extremely limited. Central to those studies is a focus on the sociopolitical opposition expressed towards as also the contestation caused by 'new' mosques. Within this literature however—and similar to that relating to Muslim women and men—there is a clear overlap between

C. Allen, *Reconfiguring Islamophobia*, Palgrave Hate Studies,
https://doi.org/10.1007/978-3-030-33047-7_7

the understanding of mosques and other physical structures and the 'problems' associated with Islam and Muslims (Allen, 2017). In this way, it would seem that physical structures have the potential to serve a function extremely similar to the hijab, niqab, beard and so on. Accordingly, in addition to functioning as markers of Muslimness but so too would it seem that the physical structures associated with Muslims and Islam confer legitimacy on the sociopolitical problematisation of Muslims and Islam, as before, conferring legitimacy on the normative truths. This is evident in the studies of Cesari (2005) who, in the French setting, notes how the contestation associated with mosques reflect wider sociopolitical tensions attributed to Muslims and Islam in the public and political spaces. Similarly too Saint-Blancat and di Friedberg (2005), arguing that opposition to mosques in Italy links to broader questions about the presence of Muslims in the country. Landman and Wessels (2005) in the Netherlands and McLoughlin (2005) in the UK look slightly more broadly, inferring how local, regional and national contestation reflect increasingly pervasive discourses that exist at the transnational level, not least the Islamification of Europe.

The best illustration of this symbolic problematisation is in Switzerland however and the 57 per cent majority that voted in 2009 to ban the building of minarets. At the time of the vote, of the nearly 150 mosques in Switzerland only 4 had minarets attached to them (Stüssi, 2008). For Nussbaum (2012), the referendum can be seen to afford an unprecedented insight into how minor and at times irrelevant 'problems' associated to Muslims and Islam are rapidly transformed into public crises that are seen to have profound national, political and cultural significance. For Stüssi (2008), the outcome of the referendum has to be understood as being wholly symbolic: serving to empower those who had concerns, fears and anxieties about Muslims and Islam to act accordingly, to do 'something'. Undoubtedly little more than a hollow victory, the successful halting of the potential building of minarets in Swiss towns and cities was for those supporting it was a small but wholly significant step in the much larger process of halting Muslims and Islam from Islamifying—and thereby, taking over—the country. For some, it is highly likely this was also a significant step in the halting of Muslims and Islam taking over Europe more widely.

Noting Hargreaves' (2015) previously considered concerns, while such processes are problematic in that they infer the embeddedness of certain normative truths about Muslims and Islam in the public and political spaces, the Swiss referendum does not necessarily fit with the 'real' and tangible Islamophobia being investigated here. In this respect, Allievi's (2009) analysis is extremely useful. For him, mosques function as convenient symbols against which those who wish to vent their anger and hatred of Muslims and Islam are able to do so. In line with the earlier observation then, mosques function similar to the hijab or niqab as regards Muslim women and beards and certain attire as regards Muslim men. Because of this, attacks and crimes targeting mosques—and other physical structures associated with Muslims and Islam—are not only similar to those targeting Muslim men and Muslim women but so too do they fit within the definition of real and tangible manifestations of Islamophobia set out previously. Like those crimes and attacks targeting Muslim men and women, then crimes and attacks targeting mosques and other physical structures can be legitimately justified as 'real' and tangible and therefore appropriate for further consideration in the context of this book.

'Muslims Out of Britain': Graffiti and the Radical Right

Tell MAMA (2017) employ a six-fold categorisation process for attacks and crimes targeting mosques: graffiti, smashed windows, desecration, violent break-ins, arson and bombings. A more appropriate approach however might be one that reflects the low-level-high-level categorisation evident in the existing literature and referred to in previous chapters. In this way, graffiti, smashed windows and desecration might be best regarded as 'low level' while violent break-in, arson and bombings 'high level'. As with attacks and crimes targeting individuals, it is right to stress that low level does not necessarily mean low impact (Allen, Isakjee, & Ögtem-Young, 2013). In the context of physical structures, attacks and crimes involving graffiti are useful for illustrating this. While low level, the potential reach and subsequent impact of graffiti goes way beyond those who first experienced it and subsequently reported it. Accordingly, if that graffiti includes a threatening message—common in much of the graffiti experienced by the respondents engaged here—so that threat has the potential to impact a much greater number of people: all those who see it and identify with the group targeted. It is for this reason that those who seek to dismiss out of hand such low-level occurrences are wrong to do so (Malik, 2005).

A recurrent feature of the mosque graffiti experienced by respondents made an explicit link between Muslims or Islam to notions of evil, violence and terrorism. Like the content of Islamophobia that was individually targeted, some graffiti also included messages that demanded Muslims *go home*. Here again, Muslims—and by extension, the religion of Islam—were not seen as belonging or being a part of who 'we' are. Not all the graffiti however contained or sought to convey a message. As one respondent explained, their mosque merely had paint thrown over its external walls. Another experienced similar albeit with the addition of eggs and rotten tomatoes having been thrown along with paint. Particularly prominent and of concern to respondents was the incorporation of radical right terminology and emblems into the graffiti. Most common were references to the English Defence League (EDL) and National Front (NF), common also was the inclusion of swastikas. As one respondent explained, the graffiti at their mosque incorporated both a clear anti-Muslim message with a far-right emblem: 'Muslims out of Britain' adjacent to a swastika. While so, the respondent was not entirely convinced that the radical right were involved. As he explained, '*I genuinely can't tell if these people necessarily belong to a far-right group…it only takes one or two individuals to commit these kinds of incidents*'.

Not all respondents were this sceptical however. Another respondent was absolutely convinced the radical right were involved in an incident that saw a number of windows being smashed while evening prayers were underway at the mosque. As the respondent recalled, on hearing glass being broken, a number of the worshippers ran outside where they found three men who were described as '*causing a commotion*'. This included personally abusing worshippers and shouting insults about Muslims and Islam more generally. The three men then came across some old chairs and a table being stored at the side of the mosque. Having done so, the respondent spoke about how two of the men threw the large table through a large window causing the glass to shatter and spray across the inside of the prayer hall, hitting some of those who had remained inside. As the respondent went on, they were '*members of the EDL…I know it, they were for sure*'. In justifying this, he said that EDL members had been targeting the mosque for a while, uploading a number of abusive videos to the internet among others. Stressing his unequivocal perception that the EDL were culpable, he claimed they had been behind a number of other attacks too, targeting Muslim-owned shops and young Muslims being intimidated and verbally abused on their way home from school.

High-Level Hate: Pig's Blood and Bombs

Some of the respondents spoke about experiencing hate crimes involving desecration. This typically involved positioning pig meat, pig's blood or parts of pig's carcasses in or around mosques or similarly daubing it. Underpinning this type of incident is the view that pig meat and blood is haram (forbidden) for Muslims and thereby unclean. From those engaged, two respondents recounted incidents involving pig's blood smeared over the doors to their respective mosques. Having been increasing in number for a decade and a half, one of the first recorded incidents occurred in 2002 when a mosque was attacked as 'revenge' for the 9/11 attacks (BBC News, 2002). Elsewhere, individual Muslim families have been similarly targeted (Allen, 2014, 2015). What is maybe most interesting is how the underlying message of this type of act can be drawn on to illustrate resonance between 'real' Islamophobia and that which occurs in the political spaces. During his 2016 election campaign, President Trump told supporters a story about a US general who allegedly slaughtered 49 Muslims using bullets dipped in pig's blood (Embury-Dennis, 2019). Describing the 49 killed as 'terrorists', there appears to be no historical evidence for the story. Nonetheless, the symbolic function afforded by pig's blood—and the meanings such conveys—transcends the public, political and 'real'. While some contestation between these clearly exists, there is clear resonance also.

As with the high-level nature of desecration, other respondents experienced similarly high-level hate crimes. One of those included an arson attack on a mosque timed to coincide with communal prayers. The respondent said that at the time of the attack, she had been outside the mosque and recalled how she had seen a firebomb land on the roof. Immediately calling 999, she said she tried to evacuate the worshippers gathered inside. While the damage caused was eventually minimal, the respondent admitted '*it could have been far worse...especially if we'd not been outside the mosque and everyone had not acted so quickly*'. Talking about the fear and anxiety it prompted among the local Muslim community, she said that most worrying for her was the fact the perpetrators knew '*it was a mosque and that we use it at that time for praying*'. For her, this was especially chilling, hitting home the reality of Islamophobia: '*they really can't like us...I don't know why, what do we do wrong in the local area? We just go and pray and go home*'. Another respondent experienced a similar situation, a perpetrator trying to set fire to the mosque's doors during evening prayers.

When they failed to light the doors—which were made of wood—the perpetrator gathered a pile of old paper and scraps that had been nearby and tried to set fire to them. Causing no damage whatsoever, the respondent said that it was only noticeable by the smell of burning when he left the mosque.

Another arson attack occurred overnight when the mosque in question was closed and empty. In this particular instance, the fire destroyed more than two-thirds of the building. As the respondent rhetorically put it, '*the attack was really shocking, why would someone go to such lengths? What drives them to do such things?*' Costing thousands of pounds to repair and subsequently rebuild, the respondent spoke about how this had not been the first arson attack at the site. Previously, it would seem the mosque had been broken into at which point the perpetrators '*made a big pile of stuff and tried to set it alight. It was deliberate…Alhamdulillah it didn't ignite this time though*'. Another arson attack also occurred albeit after the perpetrators had broken into the mosque. As the respondent explained, the two young men that were subsequently arrested had entered the mosque through a couple of smashed windows. Once inside, she said, they started a fire just behind the main doors. In spite of having ignited, the fire failed to spread causing minimal damage to the door frame and part of its frontage.

Two respondents also experienced bomb attacks at their respective mosques, neither of which were able to recall any previous attacks or incidents. While so, the two attacks were extremely similar with explosive devices left outside the mosque in order to detonate them at a time when worshippers would have been either inside or arriving for prayers. At the first, the detonation coincided with early evening prayers; at the second, the same coincided with Friday prayers, a time when the mosque was at its most full. Maybe somewhat surprisingly, despite both bombs detonating, there were no injuries at either. As regards the first, the respondent spoke about how '*we heard a loud noise but couldn't see anything and just thought that someone was messing around…so we didn't do anything about it*'. As he went on, '*why would you ever think a bomb had been left outside?*' At the latter, the respondent said that worshippers were only aware of the bomb when they found an unusual amount of debris in the car park and road nearby. As he added, it was only after the police investigation that worshippers accepted the debris was the result of detonated explosives. A similar response was evident among worshippers at the first mosque. As the respondent explained, the general response was one of incredulity. It was only after the police's forensic officers showed him and those working at the mosque the remains of the bomb did they really appreciate the seriousness of the attack.

Reflecting on the Causes: 'Too Depressing to Even Think About'

More so than those individually targeted, respondents that experienced Islamophobia targeting physical structures were rather more reflective: trying to rationalise and explain why what happened duly happened. Among them, there was some disagreement however. For the majority, there was a sense that they were the direct consequence to different terror-related incidents involving Muslims. A handful of respondents were less certain however, not necessarily having or putting forward any alternative. One respondent's explanation was however particularly insightful. For him, he preferred to see the attack on his mosque as being unprovoked and perpetrated by opportunists. As he went on, '*if not, it's just too depressing to even think about...it would make me want to lose faith in humanity*'. While another respondent seemed to suggest similar, the respondent's view did waver slightly. After some time and somewhat reluctantly, she said it was likely that in the mind of the perpetrators there was a link between Muslims who commit atrocities and the '*ordinary Muslims who use the mosque and live their lives round here*'. As she went on, there was a chance that targeting her mosque was the '*result of prejudices and anger that some groups have in society towards Muslims*'.

Among respondents who made a more explicit or direct link, there was however some divergence. One respondent for example, suggested '*anybody would turn to the idea that [any hate crime] was a backlash to an incident*' before adding '*it could just be a random attack or a revenge on someone or something that is not connected to anything*'. As with the resonance between the stories of Trump and the realities of locally focused hate crimes previously, another respondent was clear that events occurring nationally and internationally were present in the minds of those perpetrating the local attacks. As one respondent agreed, '*it was definitely a reaction to recent events*'. Among respondents, a number of terror-related incidents were cited incidents as potential catalysts for the attacks. These included the murder of Lee Rigby in London, Charlie Hebdo attacks in Paris, the emergence of Islamic State and the Manchester Arena bomb attack. For one, this was the only explanation. As he went on, his mosque had always enjoyed good relations with local non-Muslim communities and so it would need something '*utterly horrific*' to change that. Another respondent voiced similar, '*because the incidents are so horrific…they cause a backlash and antagonise a lot of people*'. The stark difference in response between those experiencing individual Islamophobia and those experiencing Islamophobia targeting physical structures was at times then, somewhat different.

The articulation of another respondent was particularly pertinent. For her, the targeting of her mosque was '*a form of hatred towards Islam*'. As she went on, the mosque '*was targeted…because the building is a symbol of Islam*'. By making this link, she was suggesting exactly Allievi's (2009) premise that physical structures including associated with Muslims and Islam like mosques perform a symbolic function. Combined with her statement that mosques—as indeed other physical structures—provide an *easy target* for those seeking revenge against Muslims and their religion, so it is possible to argue that these can be understood as markers of Muslimness. As set out previously and in line with Allen (2017), it is also likely that the symbolic function mosques and other physical structures perform do so through embodying normative truths: thereby playing out the problematisation of Muslims and the religion of Islam. This was evident in how a number of respondents spoke about the problematisation of Muslims and Islam in the contemporary setting. As one respondent put it, this was clear in how '*the media and authorities constantly create negative portrayals of Muslims*'. Going on, he made the link between the media and those who might perpetrate hate crimes: '*people are simple…they look at headlines and they make their minds up for them*' thereby resulting in '*creating Islamophobia*'.

According to another respondent, Islamophobia was the consequence of a process whereby people '*want a scapegoat*'. For him, this was especially true in relation to terror-related incidents. At these times he added, a '*sort of vulnerability*' becomes quickly apparent among Muslim communities. As he explained, '*not only does it feel that the [Muslim] community is attacked collectively for a crime that is committed by someone else…it also feels they are under siege and held responsible for what happened wherever that may be*'. Accordingly, '*the whole [Muslim] community has been punished*'. Here again, the notion of normative truths is evident, evident in the way respondents perceive that certain meanings and understandings about Muslims and Islam inform the wider sociopolitical consensus. A key element of this being that Muslims and Islam are a largely unidimensional and wholly homogeneous entity attributed with a series of negative and stereotypical characteristics. For this reason, not only do all Muslims appear—and at times, feel—unquestionably culpable but so too does it go some way to explain how those experiencing this type of Islamophobia hate crime seek to rationalise their experience.

Real and Tangible: Unreal Criticisms and Contestation

Across this and in the earlier two chapters, a real and tangible Islamophobia has not only been established but more importantly, evidenced. This is quite different 'proving' Islamophobia or its existence, something this book did not aim to achieve. Aligned with the definition set out previously, the experiences considered here illustrate how Islamophobia is manifested, how it is expressed and how it impacts not only those who encounter it first-hand but so too their families, friends and communities. While there are some discrepancies in official data not least knowledge that up to 70 per cent of Islamophobic hate crimes are never reported to the police or any other statutory agency (Allen, 2014), the evidence here shines a spotlight on the type of Islamophobia that is routinely and regularly experienced by ordinary people going about their ordinary who happen to be Muslim and are duly targeted for hate on the basis of that recognition and identification. To this extent, Islamophobia is real and tangible. Irrespective of criticism or contestation, this is unequivocal and unarguable. If so, why then does Islamophobia remain criticised and contested? Maybe more pertinently, what are those who criticise and contest focusing on—and subsequently ignoring—when they dismiss Islamophobia out of hand or even, that it is a mere 'fiction'? Likewise, what exactly is it that those who are endeavouring to establish a consensually agreed working definition are actually trying to define? Is it the real and tangible Islamophobia evident here or is it something rather more nebulous? Are they trying to define that which critics claim does not exist all the while ignoring the hard evidence that does? It is as if these two constituencies are solely communicating with each other and no-one else.

To understand this more fully, it is important to revisit the criticisms and contestations routinely put forward and previously considered. As regards the UK Government, a spokesperson stated that the working definition—or indeed any other definition—was not being adopted on the basis it did not receive broad acceptance (Allen, 2019). Irrespective of whether broadly accepted or not, clearly both the Government and the APPG on British Muslims seem to have overlooked that not only is Islamophobia—at least in the form of hate crime—real and tangible but so too does the Government's own data evidence this. The focus on the definition then seems to negate if not completely ignore the evidence both already have to hand. Another criticism was that the proposed working definition had potential to cause confusion among police officers tasked with enforcing it while also limiting free speech (Dodd, 2019). What is interesting is that police forces across the country already record religiously motivated—including Islamophobically motivated—hate crime in the same way they do other forms of hate crime. That they already do this—and to some success—therefore weakens, if not entirely undermines, such a concern. Here again, both the Government and those endeavouring to establish a definition appear to be ignoring the fact that such an argument can be proven to be quite insignificant and without substance. Police forces are already doing what critics claim they will not subsequently be able to.

Another criticism was that the working definition had the potential to limit free speech (Dodd, 2019). As regards the real and tangible Islamophobia evidenced here, it is difficult to see how or where this might occur. Whether considering the experience of women, men or physical structures targeted by Islamophobic hate crime, at no time did matters of free speech come into focus, neither directly nor indirectly. In this respect, it would seem that the Islamophobia referred to as regards the potential to limit free speech has little to do with Islamophobia that is real and tangibly manifested. The same would appear true of the claim that a definition of Islamophobia would potentially undermine certain counter-terrorism powers. While some respondents highlighted the link between their experiences of Islamophobic hate crime and a backlash or revenge for certain terrorism-related atrocities, it is difficult to understand how this might undermine certain counter-terrorism powers. Rather than rooted in the evidence relating to real and tangible manifestations of Islamophobia, such criticisms and concerns are rather more rooted in the conflation of Islamophobia with various sociopolitical issues attributed to Muslims and Islam and the problematisation that ensues. Akin to how Hargreaves (2015) criticises some scholarly studies for conceiving Islamophobia as an all-encompassing phenomenon, one that aggregates a range of different sociopolitical issues that go beyond manifestations of discrimination, bigotry and hate, so too would this appear to be true of those criticising and contesting Islamophobia. Criticising Islamophobia for potentially damaging free speech, curtailing academic and journalistic freedom, damaging social cohesion and introducing blasphemy laws by the 'backdoor' would all seem to function in this way (Allen, 2019)—none seemingly having any impact or relevance whatsoever to the real and tangible manifestations evidenced here.

If therefore, critics—like some scholarly studies—are conflating a whole range of different sociopolitical issues that problematise Muslims and the religion of Islam with Islamophobia, to what extent are those attempting to define Islamophobia seeking to put forward a definition that too is not only equally all-encompassing but also inappropriately so? Maybe then it was right to state that the working definition put forward by the APPG on British Muslims was too vague (Allen, 2019). Given that what is being attempted to be defined is inappropriate and inaccurate as the definitions being proposed, to what extent has Islamophobia as a real and tangible discriminatory phenomenon been miscast and misunderstood—as also overlooked and largely ignored—in the public and political spaces? Is it possible that there is as much confusion among those seeking to establish a working definition as indeed there is among those seeking to criticise and contest? Is it possible that because Islamophobia has been so routinely conflated with a spectrum of sociopolitical issues that are variously—and at times, only tenuously—linked to the real and tangible Islamophobia evidenced here that it is now difficult to refocus the debate whether in the public, political or scholarly spaces? The following part builds on some of these questions through investigating Islamophobia in the public and political spaces.

References

Allen, C. (2014). Exploring the impact of Islamophobia on visible Muslim women victims: A British case study. *Journal of Muslims in Europe, 3*(2), 137–159.

Allen, C. (2015). 'People hate you because of the way you dress': Understanding the invisible experiences of veiled British Muslim women victims of Islamophobia. *International Review of Victimology, 21*(3), 287–301.

Allen, C. (2017). Islamophobia and the problematization of mosques: A critical exploration of hate crimes and the symbolic function of "old" and "new" mosques in the United Kingdom. *Journal of Muslim Minority Affairs, 37*(3), 294–308.

Allen, C. (2019). *Islamophobia defined*. London: Religion Media Centre.

Allen, C., Isakjee, A., & Ögtem-Young, Ö. (2013). *Maybe we are hated: The experience and impact of anti-Muslim hate on British Muslim women*. Birmingham: University of Birmingham.

Allievi, S. (2009). *Conflicts over mosques in Europe: Policy issues and trends*. London: Alliance Publishing Trust.

BBC News. (2002, August 6). Guard dumped pigs' heads at mosque. *BBC England*. Retrieved from http://news.bbc.co.uk/1/hi/england/2176553.stm

Cesari, J. (2005). Mosques in French cities: Towards the end of a conflict? *Journal of Ethnic and Migration Studies, 31*(6), 1025–1043.

Dodd, V. (2019). Police chiefs in row over definition of Islamophobia. *The Guardian*. Retrieved from https://www.theguardian.com/news/2019/may/15/police-chiefs-in-row-over-definition-of-islamophobia

Driessen, G., & Merry, M. S. (2006). Islamic schools in the Netherlands: Expansion or marginalization? *Interchange, 37*(3), 201–223.

Dwyer, C., & Meyer, A. (1995). The institutionalisation of Islam in the Netherlands and in the UK: The case of Islamic schools. *Journal of Ethnic and Migration Studies, 21*(1), 37–54.

Embury-Dennis, T. (2019). Trump tells fake story about US general slaughtering 49 Muslims using bullets dipped in pig's blood, in resurfaced video. *The Independent*. Retrieved from https://www.independent.co.uk/news/world/americas/us-politics/trump-muslims-general-pershing-pigs-blood-video-a8829676.html

Hargreaves, J. (2015). Half a story? Missing perspectives in the criminological accounts of British Muslim communities, crime and the criminal justice system. *British Journal of Criminology, 55*(1), 19–38.

Jaschok, M., & Shui, S. J. (2013). *The history of women's mosques in Chinese Islam*. Routledge.

Landman, N., & Wessels, W. (2005). The visibility of mosques in Dutch towns. *Journal of Ethnic and Migration Studies, 31*(6), 1125–1140.

Malik, K. (2005). *Transcript of Kenan Malik's film "Are Muslims Hated?"* Retrieved December 12, 2016, from http://www.kenanmalik.com/tv/c4_islamophobia.html

McLoughlin, S. (2005). Mosques and the public space: Conflict and cooperation in Bradford. *Journal of Ethnic and Migration Studies, 31*(6), 1045–1066.

Nussbaum, M. C. (2012). *the new religious intolerance: Overcoming the politics of fear in an anxious age*. Cambridge, MA: Belknap Press of Harvard University Press.

Rashid, H. M., & Muhammad, Z. (1992). The Sister Clara Muhammad schools: Pioneers in the development of Islamic education in America. *The Journal of Negro Education, 61*(2), 178–185.

Saint-Blancat, C., & di Friedberg, O. S. (2005). Why are mosques a problem? Local politics and fear of Islam in Northern Italy. *Journal of Ethnic and Migration Studies, 31*(6), 1083–1104.

Scriver, P. (2004). Mosques, ghantowns and cameleers in the settlement history of colonial Australia. *Fabrications, 13*(2), 19–41.

Stüssi, M. (2008). Banning of minarets: Addressing the validity of a controversial Swiss popular initiative. *Religion & Human Rights, 3*(2), 135–153.

Tell MAMA. (2017). *Beyond the incident: Outcomes for victims of anti-Muslim prejudice*. London: Faith Matters.

PART III

Political Approaches to Islamophobia

CHAPTER 8

That Which Must Not Be Named: Islamophobia and New Labour

Following on from the preceding part, there would appear to be little rationale for Islamophobia's contestation in the public and political spaces given the overwhelming evidence that it is both real and indeed tangible. As alluded to in the opening chapter, it would therefore seem that there is something of a significant disparity between a publicly and politically conceived Islamophobia and the Islamophobia experienced by real people in real situations. While one must admire the endeavours of the APPG on British Muslims and others that have contributed to the process of trying to find a definition that somehow spans or at least minimises this disparity, it is clear that no definition is in fact going to provide the 'solution' to the 'problem'. In fact, a recent incident referring to its definition precisely illustrates this point. During the period of time when the Government was considering whether to adopt the APPG's proposed working definition, *The Sun* newspaper columnist Trevor Kavanagh wrote a piece titled 'Hidden Women' (Kavanagh, 2019). At odds with the rest of his column—primarily focusing on Brexit, Britain's planned exit from the European Union—Kavanagh criticised two recent news reports. The first he alleged stated that there had been attempts in Iran to forbid men from looking at women during the month of Ramadan. The second alleged that in Afghanistan, there had been calls to ban music involving women on the basis of its potential to provoke 'sexual excitement'. Despite neither having any clear nor direct relevance to Britain, Kavanagh concluded his piece with the following sentence: 'Meanwhile in Britain, the Government is

C. Allen, *Reconfiguring Islamophobia*, Palgrave Hate Studies,
https://doi.org/10.1007/978-3-030-33047-7_8

considering adopting a definition of Islamophobia which could make criticism of Islam a hate crime' (Kavanagh, 2019).

Shortly after, the Centre for Media Monitoring (CfMM) lodged a formal complaint about the column with the Independent Press Standards Organisation (IPSO), the UK's independent regulator for most British-based newspapers and magazines. Set up by the Muslim Council of Britain, the CfMM—which challenges inaccurate stories and reports about Muslims and Islam—claimed the article was inaccurate and misleading. Upholding the complaint, IPSO requested *The Sun* newspaper to acknowledge its error. Refusing to publicly state any wrongdoing, the regulator subsequently forced *The Sun* to do so, albeit without the apology the CfMM would have liked. In it, *The Sun* stated that 'at the time of publication, no such laws had been proposed by the Government. Rather, the Government was considering a definition of Islamophobia which, in the opinion of the columnist, risked making criticism of religion a hate crime' (The Sun, 2019). Irrespective of the columnist's opinion, there is no doubt that what was stated was inaccurate and extremely misleading. While impossible to gauge the extent to which this opinion was deliberate—it would seem that it was—the piece is maybe even more problematic for the underlying message it clearly conveys. As with some of the content of verbal abuse experienced by Muslim men and women evidenced previously, the message being conveyed is that, without any doubt whatsoever, all Muslims are one and the same. Accordingly, in the same way, Muslims are trying to impose what are being presented as unreasonable demands in Iran and Afghanistan, so those Muslims that are here in Britain—and 'the West' more widely—will try and impose similar demands on 'us' and how 'we' live 'our' lives. Going beyond that, the article more worryingly infers that the British Government's plans to introduce legislation to afford protection to Muslims from discrimination and hate will catalyse this process, thereby strengthening the hand of Muslims to—either directly or indirectly—introduce 'their' laws and way of life over 'ours'.

Two important points emerge. The first is that, had the working definition been adopted by the Government when this was published, what function would it have served in this instance? Despite the fact that the column was about the proposed definition, the complaint was not only upheld but so too was a correction demanded by the IPSO. In this respect, it is not clear what other—or indeed better—outcome the adoption of any working definition could have achieved. While mere speculation, the only other function the adoption of the definition might have performed is to have stopped Kavanagh from being able to make such a claim in the first place. For this to happen though, there would have been a need to have legislation in place that made it illegal to say or allege certain things about Muslims and the religion of Islam, something those championing the definition were clearly not suggesting. That some might argue that what Kavanagh wrote was in itself Islamophobic prompts a further question about whether the working definition would have afforded any credence to such a claim. This leads to the second and the extent to which the proposed working definition—or indeed any other definition—has the potential to 'join up' the real and tangible Islamophobia with that which is evident in the public and political spaces. As regards the APPG definition, it is not necessarily clear how it might do that. While it potentially alludes to both, it concretises neither. To 'solve', therefore, the perceived 'problem', it would seem that a far more all-encompassing definition is necessary, albeit noting that adopting such an all-encompassing approach is also extremely problematic.

This and the following chapter therefore seek to investigate these and other issues in greater detail through considering how Islamophobia is not only conceived in the political and thereby public spaces but so to what political mechanisms and policy interventions have been put in place to respond and subsequently address the phenomenon. As before, the UK provides a number of unique insights that have resonance to other locations and settings, especially those where Islamophobia is currently emerging as a public and political 'problem'. The UK is also relevant, given the perception in other countries that it is at the forefront of politically responding to Islamophobia. This became apparent to the author when he was invited to participate in a round-table event in Stockholm organised by the Swedish Government's Department for Discrimination Issues in June 2014. Bringing together politicians and community activists from across Europe, it was quite unexpected the extent to which the UK was seen to be at the forefront of tackling Islamophobia. The author has experienced similarly in other contexts too, including being invited to participate as a delegate in an exchange initiative organised in 2016 as part of the US International Visitor Leadership Program between the cities of Denver in Colorado and Birmingham in the West Midlands. While surprised by the credence afforded the UK, it was also widely apparent that irrespective of whether the political mechanisms and policy interventions implemented in the UK had been positive and impacting, more did appear to be being done in the UK than elsewhere. On this basis, while the UK offers more to investigate, this does not necessarily mean that it has had the greatest or most positive impact or that it is better than elsewhere.

This and the following chapters then are structured around the different and quite distinct approaches adopted by two political party-led governments. This chapter focuses on the New Labour Government that was in place from 1997 through to 2010. The following chapter focuses on the Conservative Party, both in terms of it being the majority partner in the coalition government that was in power from 2010 through to 2015 and the consecutive Conservative-only Governments elected in 2015 and then again in 2017. At the time of writing, the Conservatives continue to form the Government of the UK, albeit without a workable majority. As before however, it is necessary to reiterate the limitations of political mechanisms and policy interventions as regards discriminatory phenomena. As a recap, such approaches typically only function to curb certain behaviours, thereby rarely ever changing public opinions, attitudes or thinking (Blakemore & Drake, 1996; Daniels & Macdonald, 2005). Because of this, rarely do such approaches address the causes of discriminatory phenomena. Adopting Bhavani, Mirza, and Meetoo's (2005) typology of intervention—formal and informal—both this and the following chapter will consider how both Governments have conceived and understood Islamophobia, what measures it has put in place to recognise and duly respond to Islamophobia and what successes—if indeed any—these have achieved.

Islamophobia: Immediately Dismissed, Worryingly Conflated

Reflecting on New Labour's approach to Islamophobia, a number of issues emerge that require further consideration The first is the lack of any meaningful political recognition afforded to Islamophobia as also the lack of any meaningful political commitment to do something about it. This was readily apparent from the outset and the publication of the CBMI report (Commission on British Muslims and Islamophobia, 1997). Launched at the House of Commons, the aforementioned Jack Straw speaking on behalf of the newly elected New Labour Government somewhat surprisingly dismissed the CBMI's call for the introduction of new legislation to protect Muslims against discrimination and hate (Allen, 2010). Instead, he announced that the Government was planning to introduce additional legislation to protect against 'racial violence'. Despite the CBMI and its report presenting Islamophobia as a distinct phenomenon, Straw—and the New Labour Government—immediately dismissed the notion of a particularistic Islamophobia in preference of conflating it with racism. Accordingly, from the moment Islamophobia entered the political and subsequently public spaces too, not only was its particularistic nature—one based on markers of Muslimness—negated but so too was it roundly dismissed. It is interesting to note how similar Straw's—and New Labour's—immediate and unequivocal dismissal of Islamophobia was with those of its critics and detractors.

The newly installed New Labour Government however was much more open to faith and religion than most of its predecessors. According to Gilliat-Ray (2004), this was apparent in former Prime Minister Tony Blair's language about 'social inclusion': going beyond material wealth and poverty to focus on issues that included citizenship and equality. So too did the emergence and greater willingness of faith groups to provide voluntary services and the economic viability that came with this make some aspects of religion appear somewhat more appealing to a political audience (Gilliat-Ray, 2004). A number of other drivers can also be seen to be relevant including: growing levels of poverty and deprivation within certain religious communities (Anwar & Bakhsh, 2003; Woodhead, 2010); the establishment of nonhistorical religious traditions in Britain and the demographic changes catalysed (Bruce, 1996; Davie, 1994); and shifts in how individuals and communities chose to identify, including by religion (Oliver-Dee, 2009). One also cannot overlook that several prominent members of the New Labour Government—including Blair—were practising Christians (Harris, Halfpenny, & Rochester, 2003). Maybe most pertinent however was the growing antipathy shown towards Muslims following the 9/11 attacks in the United States (Allen, 2005). For McLoughlin (2003), it was this more than anything else that prompted New Labour to want to engage more with the country's Muslims.

In spite of this, New Labour continued to overlook a particularistic Islamophobia in preference of a much broader and, importantly, less specific concept of religiously motivated discrimination. Consequently, New Labour introduced two policy interventions of note: one formal, the other informal. As regards the former, the introduction of the *Human Rights Act 1998* constitutionally established the freedom to religion or belief. As regards the latter, in 1999, New Labour commissioned major research into religious discrimination. The ensuing report *Religious Discrimination in England and Wales* (Weller, Feldman, & Purdam, 2001) noted that Britain's Muslims were most likely to be targeted for discrimination. Somewhat unsurprisingly, Muslim communities also felt that levels of discrimination and hate against them were increasing. As Weller—the report's lead author—has retrospectively noted, the report 'involved walking something of a political and publicity tightrope, suspended between community expectations, scientific research methodologies, the political context, the staff and perspectives of the Home Office's Research, Development and Statistics Directorate' (2006, p. 308). As he goes on, there was also a palpable disappointment among some Muslim organisations and communities that the report failed to specifically refer to Islamophobia given that it was the most prevalent phenomenon identified (Weller, 2006). Clearly, there was a reluctance—at least in some quarters—to acknowledge and subsequently name Islamophobia. The conflation referred to previously was again borne out in the report's recommendation: like Straw, calling for the need to extend race relations legislation. So too did the report recommend extending Britain's largely defunct blasphemy laws to afford protection to religions rather than people. Far from necessary to address the tangible Islamophobia experienced by Britain's Muslims, it is likely that such a recommendation merely gave its critics and detractors more 'evidence' that addressing Islamophobia was far more insidiously about protecting religions.

A 'Cancer' Left Untreated

Around the same time, the scale of the fallout from 9/11 was becoming apparent with the number of street-level attacks targeting Muslims increasing (Allen & Nielsen, 2002). In response, New Labour—via one of its ministers, John Denham—voiced concern, metaphorically suggesting that the effects of Islamophobia would be cancer-like if left untreated (Denham, 2001). While so, Denham's specific reference to 'Islamophobia' was wholly anomalous: being extremely rare for New Labour to use the term let alone refer to it in any particularistic way. This was evident in its immediate response to 9/11, formal interventions in the form of legislation being introduced that sought to protect those at risk from religiously motivated assault or abuse—albeit not specifically Muslims—via the *Anti-Terrorism, Crime and Security Act 2001*. Other formal interventions included the *Criminal Justice Act 2003* which extended sentencing provisions for offences aggravated by hostility towards a victim's religion (as well as sexual orientation or disability) and the *Racial and Religious Hatred Act 2006* which made an offence of using threatening words or behaviour with the intention of stirring up religious hatred. Here again, a broad 'religious' or 'religiously motivated' approach as opposed one that focused on what seemed to be the 'problem' was undoubtedly preferred. Despite Denham's concern, without some form of treatment, the 'cancer' was likely to spread.

While some Muslim organisations were concerned at how New Labour consistently refused to acknowledge let alone respond to the growing levels of discrimination and hate that many within their communities were increasingly experiencing, some also expressed concern about how many of the recently introduced policy interventions responding to religiously motivated discrimination and hate were incorporated within counter-terrorism and security-focused interventions (Allen, 2011). Some were equally concerned about the extent to which these same interventions also inadvertently targeted Muslims and their communities. Whether seeking to curtail and control radicalism, proscribe extremist groups or introduce new offences relating to encouraging or preparing for terrorism, first-hand engagement with a number of Muslim organisations highlighted the growing concern at how political mechanisms and, in particular, informal discursive interventions were reinforcing many of the public's fears and anxieties about Muslims and the religion of Islam. To this extent, some felt the situation worsened again after the suicide attacks on London's public transport system in July 2005 (Allen, 2010). In the public spaces, this appeared to be evident in the quite unprecedented expansion in the number of news stories and reports about Muslims and Islam in the British media. From research undertaken at the time, the number of articles in Britain's national press increased by more than 260 per cent on a decade previously (Greater London Authority, 2007). More worrying was how more than 90 per cent of those articles presented Muslims and Islam as being associated with matters of violence, conflict and terrorism. In the public spaces—as also potentially the political spaces too—the normative truths about Muslims and Islam were being regularly and routinely affirmed.

From engaging those in the political spaces, there is an argument in circulation that it was the social and political landscape rather than anything else that dictated New Labour's response to Islamophobia at the time. While so, it cannot be denied that during this period, Islamophobia and security—two disparate and distinct, albeit not entirely exclusive issues—became inextricably linked in both public and political spaces. Not only did this result in any acknowledgement of a particularistic Islamophobia being subsumed, if not entirely lost, in discourses about security but also more importantly—and more worryingly—Islamophobia was understood as being consequential of terrorism and the atrocities caused. In its most crass form, the view that was implicitly conveyed in conversations was that 'when Muslims stop blowing themselves up, so too will Islamophobia stop'. It is worth noting that the author has heard much the same being conveyed by Muslims while engaging with political actors at a range of different levels. To reinforce this view, the last recorded reference to Islamophobia by New Labour can be seen to be telling. In an interview for *The Muslim News*, the then Prime Minister Gordon Brown stated that if New Labour were to win the forthcoming general election, it was determined to address Islamophobia by attributing it the importance it clearly needed. In isolation, such a commitment should be welcomed. In the context of the interview however, Brown made that same commitment while proposing the need for more stringent formal counter-terror interventions and making the case for Britain's Muslim communities to 'do more' (Allen, 2017).

Islamophobically Motivated Versus Religiously Motivated

In New Labour's latter years, a number of additional formal interventions extended existing equalities legislation to include protection against discrimination based on one's religion, belief or none. Lauded as a 'radical change' by Riddell and Watson (2011, p. 191), this legislative protection was incorporated under the *Equality Act 2006*, having been further strengthened by the *Equality Act 2010* a few years later. Building on the *European Employment Equality (Religion or Belief) Regulations 2003*—affording protection in employment against discrimination, harassment and victimisation—the 2006 act also legislated for the creation of the Equality and Human Rights Commission (EHRC), a public body responsible for the promotion and enforcement of equality and non-discrimination. As with Weller's research previously, some Muslim organisations and activists expressed dismay that Islamophobia had once again been sidelined given the failure of the EHRC to specifically acknowledge Islamophobia (Allen, 2013). While it was specifically referred to in one EHRC report, there was scant recognition of the prevalence or scale of the phenomenon, preferring instead to note that it was problematic

(Woodhead, 2010). While it is possible that each of these instances were inadvertent and unrelated, for whatever reason, there existed a general reluctance—possibly, antipathy—towards acknowledging Islamophobia as being specific and thereby distinct.

What impact, if indeed any, the paucity of acknowledgment for Islamophobia as a specific phenomenon had is questionable. As research published at the end of New Labour's term shows, over its 13 years in government, the number of people who felt Muslims were likely to be discriminated against or experience hate had grown significantly. To this extent, 83 per cent felt that the levels of discrimination and hate Muslims experienced were higher than five years beforehand (Allen, 2013). Concurrently, public attitudes towards Muslims and Islam had deteriorated. As the 2009–10 British Social Attitudes Survey evidenced, Muslims at the end of New Labour's time in government were the least popular religious communities in the UK. So too would more than half of people be bothered by the building of a large mosque near to where they live (National Centre for Social Research, 2010). Comparatively, only 15 per cent said they would feel similar if a large church was being built. While the findings are not Islamophobic per se, they clearly illustrate how Muslims and the religion of Islam were largely perceived and understood in the public and political spaces at the time. So too was this evident in the experience of British Muslims, who at the time felt they were the most likely minority group to be a victim of street-level hate crime (Allen, 2013). Despite the introduction of a number of formal interventions—including extending the equalities framework—Muslims were also the most likely to feel that more was needed as regards tackling discrimination and hate (Allen, 2013).

While Brown latterly stated that New Labour had always been committed to addressing Islamophobia (Allen, 2017), it is difficult to evidence this in any tangible way. This is because in little under a decade and a half, New Labour introduced neither political mechanisms nor any formal or informal policy interventions that were designed to address or respond to Islamophobia with any specificity. Neither, it has to be stated, did it make any real or conclusive effort to afford Islamophobia any real or credible acknowledgement or recognition. Evidenced by dismissals that began with Straw at the launch of the CBMI report, New Labour was clearly unconvinced of Islamophobia as either a particularistic or distinct discriminatory phenomenon. For this reason, its preferred approach throughout was focusing on and responding to discrimination and hate on the basis of broad markers of religion, belief or none. While these had the potential to include markers of Muslimness, New Labour would have been well aware that increase in religiously motivated discrimination and hate evident across its term in government was mere proxy for Islamophobia. That extending the existing equalities framework stands testament to the importance attributed to tackling discrimination and hate by New Labour makes its dismissals of Islamophobia even more perplexing. Whether it felt that addressing the 'problem' broadly would provide the 'solution' specifically is one possible interpretation. Nonetheless, it overlooks the fact that those within the political spaces—as experienced by the author—were well aware that the levels of tangible Islamophobia were increasing.

Islamophobia: An Unspoken Reality

Most telling however is how New Labour rarely named let alone spoke about Islamophobia. When it did, there was a clear disparity between Denham's early interpretation and Brown's more latterly understanding. From this, a number of points for further consideration emerge. The first is that, even if Islamophobia's framing within counter-terrorism and security had been incidental, it conveyed the misrepresentative and misguided political message that not only was Islamophobia somehow consequential of terrorism but so too were Muslims and the religion of Islam both inextricably bound up in matters of terrorism and security. The second is that if Islamophobia's framing within counter-terrorism and security was rather more deliberate and pernicious, to what extent did it merely serve the function posited by Hall and O'Shea (2013) that political discourses achieve little more than to convince us 'what we already think', here about Muslims and Islam? Drawing upon the concept of normative truths, not only did this reaffirm the association of Muslims and Islam with violence and terrorism but so too serve as a constant reminder to the threat Muslims and Islam are seen to pose. As regards the third, to what extent were the few mentions of Islamophobia—notably Brown's—little more than a bartering device? To this extent, was it merely reiterating the 'stop blowing yourself up' dichotomy referred to previously: demanding Muslim communities do more about terrorism and extremism if it expects the Government to act to stop Islamophobia?

Failing to acknowledge let alone respond to Islamophobia as a real and tangible phenomenon, New Labour also failed to address the thinking that underpins the perpetration of those same tangible manifestations.

Accordingly, it failed to 'join up' the conception of Islamophobia that exists in the public and political spaces with Islamophobia as a real and tangible phenomenon. In this respect, Islamophobia remained somewhat abstract if not understood to be a 'problem' of Muslims rather than anyone else. So too was little done to challenge the view that Islamophobia and those lobbying for government to do more had a rather more pernicious—and thereby suspicious—agenda. In this way, New Labour's approach resonated with how critics and detractors conceived and subsequently questioned, attacked or dismissed Islamophobia. That New Labour afforded it such little specific recognition or acknowledgement let alone introduce interventions to respond to it can only have strengthened the hand of those seeking to undermine the oft overlooked yet vitally important understanding that Islamophobia is unequivocally real and tangible.

References

Allen, C. (2005). From race to religion: The new face of discrimination. In T. Abbas (Ed.), *Muslim Britain: Communities under pressure*. London, UK: Zed Books.

Allen, C. (2010). Fear and loathing: The political discourse in relation to Muslims and Islam in the British contemporary setting. *Politics and Religion Journal, 4*(2), 221–236.

Allen, C. (2011). 'We don't do God': A critical retrospective of New Labour's approaches to 'religion or belief' and 'faith'. *Culture and Religion, 12*(3), 259–275.

Allen, C. (2013). Passing the dinner table test: Retrospective and prospective approaches to tackling Islamophobia in Britain. *SAGE Open, 3*(2).

Allen, C. (2017). Political approaches to tackling Islamophobia: An 'insider/outsider' analysis of the British Coalition Government's approach between 2010–15. *Social Sciences, 6*(3), 77.

Allen, C., & Nielsen, J. S. (2002). *Summary report on Islamophobia in the EU after 11 September 2001*. Vienna: EUMC.

Anwar, M., & Bakhsh, Q. (2003). *British Muslims and state policies*. Coventry, UK: Centre for Research in Ethnic Relations.

Bhavani, R., Mirza, H. S., & Meetoo, V. (2005). *Tackling the roots of racism: Lessons for success*. Bristol: Policy Press.

Blakemore, K., & Drake, R. F. (1996). *Understanding equal opportunity policies*. New York: Prentice Hall Professional Technical Reference.

Bruce, S. (1996). *Religion in the modern world: From cathedrals to cults*. Oxford: Oxford University Press.

Commission on British Muslims and Islamophobia. (1997). *Islamophobia: A challenge for us all*. London: Runnymede Trust.

Daniels, K., & Macdonald, L. A. C. (2005). *Equality, diversity and discrimination*. London: Chartered Institute of Personnel and Development.

Davie, G. (1994). *Religion in Britain since 1945: Believing without belonging*. Oxford, UK: Basil Blackwell.

Denham, J. (2001, September 29). Keynote address. *Exploring Islamophobia Conference*. University of Westminster, London, UK.

Gilliat-Ray, S. (2004). The trouble with 'inclusion': A case study of the faith zone at the Millennium Dome. *The Sociological Review, 52*(4), 459–477.

Greater London Authority. (2007). *The search for common ground: Muslims, non-Muslims and the UK media*. London: Greater London Authority.

Hall, S., & O'Shea, A. (2013). Common-sense neoliberalism. *Soundings, 55*(55), 9–25.

Harris, M., Halfpenny, P., & Rochester, C. (2003). A social policy role for faith-based organisations? Lessons from the UK Jewish voluntary sector. *Journal of Social Policy, 32*, 93–112.

Kavanagh, T. (2019). Hidden women. *The Sun*. Retrieved from https://www.thesun.co.uk/news/opinion/9059873/tories-dead-boris-johnson-survive/

McLoughlin, S. (2003). Islam, citizenship and civil society: "New" Muslim leaderships in the UK. In J. Cesari (Ed.), *European Muslims and the secular state in a comparative perspective* (pp. 100–124). Paris, France: Network on Comparative Research on Islam and Muslims in Europe.

National Centre for Social Research. (2010). *British social attitudes survey 2010* (26th ed.). London, UK: NatCen.

Oliver-Dee, S. (2009). *Religion and identity: Divided loyalties?* London, UK: Theos.

Riddell, S., & Watson, N. (2011). Equality and human rights in Britain: Principles and challenges. *Social Policy and Society, 10*, 193–203.

The Sun. (2019). Corrections and clarifications. *The Sun*. Retrieved from https://twitter.com/miqdaad/status/1166245228245860352/photo/1

Weller, P. (2006). Addressing religious discrimination and Islamophobia: Muslims and liberal democracies. The case of the United Kingdom. *Journal of Islamic Studies, 17*, 295–325.

Weller, P., Feldman, A., & Purdam, K. (2001). *Religious discrimination in England & Wales (Home Office research study 220)*. London, UK: Home Office.

Woodhead, L. (2010). *Religion or belief: Identifying issues and priorities*. Manchester, UK: Equality and Human Rights Commission.

CHAPTER 9

Passing the Dinner-Table Test: The Conservatives and the Political Spaces

Sayeeda Hussain Warsi—the daughter of Pakistani migrants to the UK—was the first Muslim woman to be selected by the Conservative Party as a parliamentary candidate in 2005. Despite losing in the election, Michael Howard—the then leader of the Conservative Party—appointed Warsi as Special Adviser for community relations. Soon after becoming Vice-Chair of the Conservative Party, she subsequently took on the role of Shadow Minister for Community Cohesion having been bestowed life peerage (an honour that applies for the period of one's own lifetime). As Baroness Warsi of Dewsbury, when she joined the House of Lords on 11 October 2007, she became its youngest member. Increasingly high profile—most prominently in trying to mediate for Gillian Gibbons, a British teacher prosecuted and jailed in Sudan for naming a teddy bear Muhammad (BBC News, 2007)—the then leader of the Conservative Party and Prime Minster of the newly elected Conservative-led Coalition appointed Warsi as Minister without Portfolio and Party Chair. The first Muslim woman to serve in a British Governmental Cabinet, Warsi made the headlines by attending her first ministerial meeting wearing a shalwar kameez, a traditional South Asian style of attire.

For some, Warsi was—and continues to be—a controversial figure. In November 2009, she was pelted with eggs during a walkabout in Luton by a group of British Muslims who accused her of not being a 'proper Muslim' and for her support of British military action in Afghanistan. As one of the protestors put it at the time, 'She is not a practising Muslim.

C. Allen, *Reconfiguring Islamophobia*, Palgrave Hate Studies,
https://doi.org/10.1007/978-3-030-33047-7_9

Clearly by looking at her she does not represent Muslims' (BBC News, 2009). The following year, the since convicted extremist preacher Anjem Choudary sought to warn her of the physical danger she could be in were she to visit certain Muslim communities in Britain. Stating that the danger went beyond mere eggs, he added:

> *She may look like a Muslim and have a Muslim-sounding name but she does not represent Islam or anyone in this country who is a Muslim. She is a 'coconut', brown on the outside but white on the inside. In fact, she is whiter than most of the other white people in government. How can she be a Muslim and support the military involvement of the British Army in Islamic countries? She is somebody who pretends to be a practising Muslim but, from her views and statements, she is clearly against Sharia. She is a disgrace and many true Muslims are angry that she claims to stand for Islam despite betraying Allah.* (Ward, 2010)

Nonetheless, Warsi continued to be outspoken on issues relevant to Muslims including condemning her Conservative Party colleague, Philip Hollobone when in 2010 he attempted to introduce legislation to ban the niqab in public spaces. Stating that all women should have the right to choose what they wear, Warsi distanced herself from the French ban—referred to in Chap. 5—given that it was not 'the British way':

> *I think I would be as offended if I was told 'actually you must wear a miniskirt to work because that's what we like women to wear' as I would be if somebody came to me and said 'we want you to be covered from head to toe because that's what we like woman to wear'.* (Nicks, 2010)

Warsi did later acknowledge however that there were some situations where wearing of the niqab was inappropriate, adding 'If I was a vegetarian I just wouldn't apply to work in an abattoir' (Bingham, 2013).

Her greatest impact however came in 2011, with a speech delivered at the University of Leicester. Specifically addressing the topic of Islamophobia, she announced that it had passed the 'dinner-table test' in today's Britain:

> *Islamophobia has now crossed the threshold of middle class respectability…For far too many people, Islamophobia is seen as a legitimate—even commendable—thing. You could even say that Islamophobia has now passed the dinner-table-test…Islamophobia should be seen as totally abhorrent—just like homophobia or Judeophobia—because any phobia is by definition the opposite of*

> *a philosophy. A phobia is an irrational fear. It takes on a life of its own and no longer needs to be justified. And all this filters through. The drip-feeding of fear fuels a rising tide of prejudice. So when people get on the tube and see a bearded Muslim, they think 'terrorist'...when they hear 'Halal' they think 'that sounds like contaminated food'...and when they walk past a woman wearing a veil, they think automatically 'that woman's oppressed'. And what's particularly worrying is that this can lead down the slippery slope to violence.* (Warsi, 2011)

For her, Islamophobia had achieved a level of conversational civility that would be deemed untenable were it to relate to anyone else except Muslims. Politically important and publicly necessary, Warsi's speech went beyond anything that had occurred previously in the UK's political spaces. Importantly, her speech signalled a new approach to Islamophobia that was delivered by the Conservative-led Coalition Government. If New Labour had failed to name let alone address about Islamophobia, Warsi's confined such an approach to the past. This newly posited approach is investigated in more detail below.

The 'Dinner-Table Test': Two Responses

Two political mechanisms were established by the Conservatives to demonstrate its new approach to Islamophobia. The first was the establishment of the All-Party Parliamentary Group on Islamophobia in 2010; the second was the establishment of the Cross-Government Working Group on Anti-Muslim Hatred ('Working Group') in 2012. While focusing specifically on Islamophobia, both reflected extremely similar mechanisms that had been previously established in relation to anti-Semitism. At the time, these developments seemed symbolic: signalling to Muslim communities as indeed others that under a Conservative-led Government, a clear and specific importance was being placed on the need to recognise and subsequently respond to Islamophobia in much the same way that anti-Semitism and indeed continued to be. Given the current Conservative Government recently decided not to adopt a working definition whilst having done so as regards anti-Semitism, one might reasonably and retrospectively question the extent to which these two discriminatory phenomena were ever seek to be akin to each other.

An interesting observation is why the APPG focused on 'Islamophobia' while the Working Group focused on 'anti-Muslim hatred'. Rather than reflecting Carr's interchangeability between Islamophobia and anti-Muslim racism, first-hand engagement suggests the use of different terminologies was due to the concerns of the Quilliam Foundation's set out in the opening chapter. To reiterate, its view was that the term Islamophobia was inappropriate and unfit for purpose given 'Islamists and Wahhabis' were exploiting it for their ideological gain (Readings, Brandon, & Phelps, 2011). If the government used it Quilliam went on, it would be a propaganda coup for Islamist extremists. What is interesting—and unexplained—is why the government sought to consult a group known to be critical of Islamophobia about the very same issue. Far from experts on the topic, Quilliam were a self-declared counter-extremism think-tank. It is also interesting that the government shifted away from using the term Islamophobia given it had already committed to using it, not least making claims to take it more seriously than its political predecessors had. Despite the recognisably new approach the Conservative-led Coalition Government were putting forward, the same contestation attributed to Islamophobia was clearly evident. So too was there the seeming underlying conflation of Islamophobia with matters relating to counter-terrorism, counter-extremism and security. It is also undeniably ironic that a critic of Islamophobia—one that is known to have contributed to its contestation in the public and political spaces—was also being endorsed, shaped and inform political thinking. While the term Islamophobia has returned term of choice in recent years, despite the seemingly unequivocal statements of Warsi, the reality was rather more unclear and questionable from very early on.

The APPG on Islamophobia: 'Little More Than a Sideshow'

Whilst early indicators the Conservative-led Coalition was embarking on a different direction than New Labour did, part of that new approach would have likely have happened irrespective of who had won the 2010 General Election. This is because the impetus for establishing an APPG on Islamophobia emanated from a closed parliamentary meeting in March 2010. Bringing together politicians from all main parties, academics, journalists, police, public servants and representatives from a number of prominent Muslim organisations (Allen, 2011), it is interesting that having been present, the author does not recall those Muslim organisations that later emerged as being integral to the APPG having attended. While launched after the general election, the establishment of the APPG was rather more independent of the Conservatives forming a Coalition Government than some at the time might have liked to infer. From November 2010 then, the APPG had a remit to: investigate the forms, manifestations and extent of discrimination against Muslims in contemporary Britain; review the effectiveness of relevant legislation; review existing mechanisms for recording anti-Muslim hate crimes; and, investigate the role of the media in fostering intolerance towards Muslims (Allen, 2017). Remarkably similar to the aims of the APPG on anti-Semitism, the APPG was intended to inform and influence the government via the Working Group that was set up within the next two years.

The APPG however was soon dogged by controversy. Following the appointment of ENGAGE as Secretariat to the APPG—a London-based Muslim organisation dedicated to improving media, civic and political engagement by that was also known as iENGAGE—a number of politicians publicly resigned from the APPG in protest (Allen, 2011). These included the APPG's Chair and Vice-Chair, Conservative parliamentarians Kris Hopkins and Lord Janner of Braunstone, respectively. Having been commissioned by Simon Hughes MP to produce a report investigating the appointment of ENGAGE and the ensuing controversy, central to the initial controversy were allegations that some affiliated to ENGAGE were 'Islamists' (Allen, 2011). While so, some of those making the allegations were also known to be highly critical and dismissive of Islamophobia, some using the term 'Islamist' pejoratively and as something of a proxy insult. Asked to resign its position, ENGAGE's response was confrontational during which time it made reference to 'Zionist' journalists, bloggers and the like while also calling Robert Halton MP a 'a nasty Israelite' (Allen, 2011, p. 36). As the report noted:

> *Most damning of all however is the realisation that Islamophobia…was completely removed from the frame within which all of the [stakeholders]… operated within. Islamophobia was lost. All [of those involved] overlooked or sidelined any focus on Islamophobia, some in preference of pursuing their own individual, organisational, political or other agendas…since its launch in November 2010 the APPG on Islamophobia has been little more than a sideshow: an unhelpful, unwanted and unnecessary distraction from giving Islamophobia the rightful, timely and necessary attention it so desperately needs.* (Allen, 2011, p. 52)

Eventually removing ENGAGE from the Secretariat role in 2011, the APPG was relaunched a year later. Again, achieving cross-party political support—albeit rather more tentatively—the APPG began devising a work programme. From early on however, it was clear that the initial impetus for the APPG had dissipated. Despite facilitating a handful of meetings over the next few years—targeting education, the media and responses to the murder of Lee Rigby in May 2013—the APPG became increasingly incoherent and lacking any apparent strategy. Tellingly, the APPG—unlike its anti-Semitism equivalent—failed to produce a single output. From first-hand engagement, it would seem that this was due to the hearings never having been recorded or transcribed. Neither was written evidence seemingly gathered in any systematic way. Without doubt, the APPG on Islamophobia was a failure. Whether the APPG on Islamophobia continues to exist in any formal capacity is unclear but one cannot ignore the similarities with the APPG on British Muslims established in the summer of 2017.

Not only did the APPG on Islamophobia fail to capitalise on the unprecedented opportunity afforded it to respond and address Islamophobia but so too did it fail to respond and address Islamophobia's contestation. There are a number of ways this can be seen to be evident. First, the APPG failed to do anything meaningful as regards addressing Islamophobia in the public or political spaces, Second, because of its lack of activity and also the controversy it attracted, Islamophobia—especially the tangible realities—was rendered invisible and irrelevant. Third, personal vendettas and petty arguments overshadowed the remit of the APPG as set out in the report of the author. Fourth, the APPG evidenced that little had changed from Sayyid's (2010) suggestion that in the political spaces Islamophobia was little more than Islamophobia a polemical mechanism: one through which to vent grievances, smugly pontificate or seek the ear of politicians at the expense of seeking to bring about real and tangible change. Fifth, the APPG did little to counter or respond to Islamophobia's critics and detractors, potential even strengthening their respective hands. And finally, the APPG served a function of convenience for all concerned. Politicians could discharge responsibility through having created and duly affording an opportunity to address Islamophobia. That it failed, they are likely to argue was not the fault of theirs. For critics and detractors, much of what ensued reinforced and reaffirmed their views and arguments. Same too for the Muslim organisations involved, who—

like the politicians—can discharge responsibility, blaming others for their failings despite having preferred to prioritise their own personal and ideological agendas over and above any wider, communal or societal need. So too can they claim to be victims in the same way critics and detractors do.

The Working Group on Anti-Muslim Hate: Another False Dawn

Launched in January 2012 following the relaunch of the APPG on Islamophobia, the Working Group was tasked with bringing together representatives from Muslim organisations, non-Muslim civil society organisations, imams and academics all of whom were invited as experts in their respective field. The Working Group also included representatives from governmental departments, the Association of Chief Police Officers and private secretaries of individual politicians with particular interest. From the terms of reference proposed at the outset, the Working Group would: make recommendations to government and others to reduce Islamophobia; respond to local or international events; review trends in anti-Muslim sentiment and hatred; increase and improve the reporting and recording of Islamophobia; and report progress to parliament (Allen, 2017). Initially active, the Working Group was quick to organise meetings with the Office of Communications (the UK's communications regulator, OFCOM), the Press Complaints Commission and Society of Editors among others: the representation of Muslims and Islam in the media clearly being prioritised.

Problems soon became apparent however not least due to the general lack of clarity about the function of the Working Group among its independent members. While some saw it as a mechanism to hold the government to account—as inferred per the terms of reference—others vehemently did not. Evidence of this was apparent when the author and two other independent members—of approximately 15—were signatories to a letter to the then Education Minister, Michael Gove criticising his response to hoax allegations of an 'Islamist takeover' in 20 state schools in the city of Birmingham; dubbed Operation Trojan Horse (Allen, 2014a). While the signatories believed Gove and the government had questions to answer, others deemed it more appropriate to 'monitor developments'. Similar disagreements emerged about the public accountability of the Working Group. Discussed at length, a minority—again including the author—believed the Working Group had a responsibility to publicly as also politically raise awareness of Islamophobia. So too could members of the Working Group offer to work with the media, thereby offering a more informed and objective voice in the public spaces. The view of the majority however was no better expressed than in the words of one member. During a heated discussion at a meeting in 2013, he said there was no good argument to convince him of 'putting my head above the parapet'. To this day, the Working Group continues to function in a largely invisible way, having no public presence whatsoever. Also to this day, it is nearly impossible to find out who currently is—or indeed has been—a member of the Working Group.

Questions also arose about decision-making in particular how these were being made and importantly, by whom. An illustrative example dates back to a research proposal presented to the Department for Communities and Local Government via the Working Group in 2013. Having identified the need improve the evidence base relating to Islamophobia, while the research was commissioned the academic members of the Working Group were overlooked as indeed were others with relevant expertise: the research being awarded to a postgraduate student from the University of Warwick with no prior knowledge of Islamophobia or associated issues. Having had the findings presented to the Working Group in May 2014, it was unanimously decided the findings should be made publicly available. Within weeks however—and outside of any meeting—that decision was overturned by an unnamed source. It was at this time the author resigned from the Working Group, describing it as impotent. As he put it, the initial expectations and hope of finally doing something meaningful about Islamophobia had 'been sadly lost, both [the Working Group] and Government having collectively failed to create the forward momentum necessary if Islamophobia was ever to have been realistically tackled' (Allen, 2014b). Another member who resigned around the same time stated:

> *the [Working Group] had no stomach to stand up and be counted in this area of work. Which begs the question. If this was the case, why were participants not removed and effective members placed in the Group who were willing to speak and go public on issues. Part of the work around tackling anti-Muslim hatred is speaking publicly about it, yet it seems that this was not the case with some members on the Group.* (Tell MAMA, 2014)

Some of the members have however claimed a number of successes when individually engaged. These include informal policy interventions such as Srebrenica Genocide Memorial Day. Held annually since 2013, this was however the result of the endeavours of a single member who had been working on establishing the day long before joining the Working Group. Other similar informal policy interventions claimed as successes include the Big Iftar and We Remember Too: the former, inviting non-Muslims to participate in the ending of the fast during the month of Ramadan; the latter, raising awareness about Muslims who fought as part of the Allied Forces in World War II. Neither were however specific to the Working Group, members instead endorsing them either individually or organisational. In common with Hall's (1979) observations about the problematic nature of similarly informal policy intervention designed to respond to racism in the 1970s, all they offer is the mere substitution of positive images or representations over and above any negative equivalent. As Hall goes on, while roundly endorsed by many as being a 'good idea' they are typically overly simplistic and lack any intrinsic value, those exposed to the positive images typically dismissing them as phoney if not wholly patronising. So too are they completely detached from the harsh realities of discriminatory phenomena that real people experience in real-life settings.

To what extent the Working Group has been successful is open to question and no doubt will continue to do so. With no outputs, no recommendations and no public presence whatsoever, few people that have not had a direct encounter with the Working Group are aware of what it does or even its existence. That it has been in existence for almost eight years at the time of writing and has survived four general elections yet is still invisible and unknown speaks volumes about the Working Group, its members as also its contribution towards responding to Islamophobia. That during its existence, the UK has witnessed the planting of three nail bombs outside mosques in the West Midlands, the murder of Mohammed Saleem and the allegations relating to Operation Trojan Horse in Birmingham, the nationally focused Punish a Muslim Day, the rampant and explicit Islamophobic rhetoric and campaigning of an emboldened radical right, the 'jokes' of Boris Johnson about niqab wearers and the terrorist attack on the Finsbury Park Mosque among others, the Working Group's silence is both telling and damning.

Analysis: Politics, Co-option and External Actors

As commendable as it was promising, Warsi's speech was unprecedented in the British political spaces. Creating high expectations that successive Conservative Governments—as part of a Coalition and as a majority—would be the first British Government to 'get it' as regards Islamophobia, the opposite was in fact rather more true. Without any doubt whatsoever, the Conservative's approach to Islamophobia was as much a failure as its much-maligned political predecessors. Having successfully put in place political mechanisms that were intended to address Islamophobia in the same way anti-Semitism had been previously, the subsequent failure feels even more disappointing. In terms of formal policy interventions, one might rightly question what successive Conservative-led Governments actually achieved. Having made such a public declaration of its priority to address Islamophobia, how then did this failure come about? It would seem that two issues are particularly pertinent in this respect. The first might be appropriately referred to as the political. Given the early discourses, it seemed—at least at the time—that there was the necessary political will to work towards addressing Islamophobia. Having participated in both the APPG and Working Group however, that political will might be questioned not least because so few politicians were supportive. For the APPG, the driving force was the parliamentarians Simon Hughes and Jack Straw. For the Working Group, Warsi performed a similar function. Having said that, it is right to note that there was representation from almost all governmental departments at Working Group meetings attended. As such, this could be interpreted as at least some semblance of cross-government support. The relevant question however is whether representation at meetings alone was enough to deliver the political leadership and will that those such as Warsi deemed necessary. Clearly, it would seem that it did not.

The second issue centres on those co-opted to support and drive forward the Conservative's approach to addressing Islamophobia. While the blueprint seemed to replicate that employed in relation to anti-Semitism, first-hand engagement highlights a number of significant differences. Among others, these include the differences that exist between Britain's Jewish and Muslim communities including sharp disparities in socio-economic status, educational attainment, demographic diversity and size, sectarian and theological differences, migration and settlement histories and the influence and impact of the geopolitical. There were practical differences too, illustrated by a meeting between the anti-Semitism and Islamophobia Working Groups in 2013. The anti-Semitism delegation comprised three members each of whom had specific expertise: one about Jewish communities, one the legal system and one religious and theological matter. In contrast, the Islamophobia delegation comprised 12 members; the number being greater had everyone been able to attend. When asked by their anti-Semitism opposite about each member's relevant expertise, few were able to articulate this in any meaningful way. These stark differences prompt a number of questions in particular about how Muslims engage in the political spaces. For example, if the anti-Semitism model was the blueprint, why were so many members recruited to the Islamophobia Working Group: was membership determined by politicians, by expertise (as initially stated) or by Muslim 'representatives' themselves? While the answer to each of these in unclear, it might be relevant to note that the majority of the Working Group's original members were affiliated to the Muslim Leadership Panel, a group seemingly formed solely to engage with government on the self-stated basis they were better equipped to do so than other groups and organisations (What Do They Know, 2012). That it also remains unclear how ENGAGE became Secretariat of the APPG not only resonates but so too suggests problematic commonalities about formal-governmental relations with Britain's Muslim communities.

Another first-hand observation was evident in a comment made by a member of the anti-Semitism Working Group. As he put it, the most important factor when engaging politically was the need to maintain a unified front. As he went on, the anti-Semitism Working Group never expressed personal, community or theological differences while engaging with politicians for fear of manipulation. That was no further from the truth among the Islamophobia Working Group. Some members appeared quite content to openly criticise certain Muslim organisations, certain 'types' of Muslims and a good number of individual Muslims during the time the author was a member. While Jones, O'Toole, DeHanas, Modood, and Meer (2015) claim Muslims who are tasked with engaging politically neither want to 'compete' against each other nor appear 'self-appointed', this was not the case when it came to the Working Group. To this extent, there were times when some members reinforced the problematisation of Muslim communities and the religion of Islam. One striking example was when one member dismissed Islamophobia as a priority, highlighting instead the need for political interventions to tackle what was referred to as the widespread homophobia and sexism rife within Muslim communities. While this may well be an issue within some Muslim communities, calling for this to be a political priority in the context and setting of a meeting about Islamophobia can be seen to make no sense at all.

When the Conservatives came into power via the Coalition Government, it did seem as though change was on the horizon. Almost a decade on and that change has been non-existent: another false dawn. As set out in this chapter, there appears to be no single factor that might be causal or explanatory. Like most other things relating to Islamophobia, the reality is rather more complex and contested also. In hindsight, the 'momentous occasion'—how the APPG was described at its launch in 2011 (Allen, 2011)—nowadays appears overblown and unnecessarily hyperbolic. That today's Prime Minister—and current leader of the *Conservative Party*—has been openly described as being Islamophobic and has been subjected to numerous calls for an internal investigation given allegations of widespread Islamophobia (Allen, 2018), it is highly unlikely that the need to address Islamophobia will be afforded any—albeit far from similar—importance in the foreseeable future of Britain's political spaces.

References

Allen, C. (2011). *A momentous occasion: A report on the All Party Parliamentary Group on Islamophobia and its secretariat*. London: All Party Parliamentary Group on Islamophobia.

Allen, C. (2014a). Operation Trojan Horse: How a hoax problematised Muslims and Islam. *Discover Society*. Retrieved from https://discoversociety.org/2014/07/01/operation-trojan-horse-how-a-hoax-problematised-muslims-and-islam/

Allen, C. (2014b). Why I Quit the Government's Anti-Muslim Hatred Working Group. *Huffington Post*. Retrieved from https://www.huffingtonpost.co.uk/dr-chris-allen/anti-muslim-hatred-working-group_b_6064866.html

Allen, C. (2017). Political approaches to tackling Islamophobia: An 'insider/outsider' analysis of the British Coalition Government's approach between 2010–15. *Social Sciences, 6*(3), 77.

Allen, C. (2018). A Summer of Islamophobia: Considering the lessons learned. *Medium*. Retrieved from https://medium.com/@mail.chrisallen/a-summer-of-islamophobia-considerations-of-the-lessons-learned-9d7b85b05014

BBC News. (2007). UK teacher jailed over teddy row. *BBC News*. Retrieved from http://news.bbc.co.uk/1/hi/world/africa/7119399.stm

BBC News. (2009). Tory Muslim peer pelted with eggs. *BBC News*. Retrieved from http://news.bbc.co.uk/1/hi/england/beds/bucks/herts/8387110.stm

Bingham, J. (2013). Banning veil would be like outlawing miniskirts, says Baroness Warsi. *Telegraph*. Retrieved from http://www.telegraph.co.uk/news/religion/10421608/Banning-veil-would-be-like-outlawing-miniskirts-says-Baroness-Warsi.html

Hall, S. (1979). *Policing the crisis: Mugging, the state, and law and order*. New York: Palgrave Macmillan.

Jones, S. H., O'Toole, T., DeHanas, D. N., Modood, T., & Meer, N. (2015). A 'system of self-appointed leaders'? Examining modes of Muslim representation in governance in Britain. *The British Journal of Politics and International Relations, 17*(2), 207–223.

Nicks, G. (2010). Conservative chairwoman: Don't ban burka. *Daily Star*. Retrieved from http://www.dailystar.co.uk/news/latest-news/147549/Conservative-chairwoman-Don-t-ban-burka

Readings, G., Brandon, J., & Phelps, R. (2011). *Islamism and language: How using the wrong words reinforces Islamist narratives*. London: Quilliam Foundation.

Sayyid, S. (2010). Thinking through Islamophobia. In S. Sayyid & A. Vakil (Eds.), *Thinking through Islamophobia: Global perspectives* (pp. 1–4). London: Hurst & Co.

Tell MAMA. (2014). The resignation of Dr Chris Allen from the Cross Govt Working Group on anti-Muslim hatred is a wake up call. *Tell MAMA*. Retrieved from https://tellmamauk.org/resignation-dr-chris-allen-cross-govt-working-group-anti-muslim-hatred-wake-call/

Ward, J. (2010). Sayeeda Warsi slammed by Islamic fundamentalists. *Daily Star*. Retrieved from http://www.dailystar.co.uk/news/latest-news/135481/Sayeeda-Warsi-slammed-by-Islamic-fundamentalists

Warsi, S. (2011). Sayeeda Warsi: University of Leicester Sir Sigmund Sternberg Lecture. *The Baroness Warsi*. Retrieved October 24, 2016, from http://sayeedawarsi.com/2011/01/20/university-of-leicester-sir-sigmundsternberg-lecture/

What Do They Know. (2012). Remit/membership of the Muslim Leadership Panel. *What Do They Know*. Retrieved from https://www.whatdotheyknow.com/request/136128/response/336750/attach/html/4/2011%2011%2014%20MLPmembers1.tif.html

CHAPTER 10

Islamophobia: Radically Reconfigured, Radically Rethought

As stated at the outset, this book aims to radically rethink and reconfigure Islamophobia. In doing so, it considers the process of conceiving and defining Islamophobia in the public, political and scholarly spaces, evidences real and tangible manifestations of Islamophobia that are experienced by Muslim women, men and communities and reflects on how successive British governments have failed to acknowledge and duly respond to Islamophobia. Central to this are the new data and findings that comprise Part II. At times shocking, these chapters alone make three necessary and important contributions. First, they contribute towards a better understanding of the experience of Islamophobia as also its impact on individual victims, their families, friends, networks and communities. Second, they contribute much-needed new knowledge about Islamophobia as experienced by Muslim men as also the experience of Islamophobia that targets physical structures associated with Muslims and Islam. To date, both have been relatively overlooked in the existing literature. Finally, they categorically refute those unfounded and typically unsubstantiated claims that question Islamophobia's legitimacy or, in the most extreme cases, that it is a mere 'fiction'.

This book is therefore intentionally disruptive: juxtaposing empirical evidence and first-hand testimonies of a real and tangible Islamophobia alongside a far more politicised and contested Islamophobia, one that typically finds form in the public and political spaces: the dichotomous tension tentatively referred to in the opening chapter. In evidencing

C. Allen, *Reconfiguring Islamophobia*, Palgrave Hate Studies,
https://doi.org/10.1007/978-3-030-33047-7_10

Islamophobia as a real and tangible discriminatory phenomenon, it goes some way to countering how that same Islamophobia is rendered quite invisible, roundly ignored and dismissed as insignificant in the public and political spaces. This is readily apparent from the analysis undertaken in Parts I and III. However, that is not and indeed cannot be allowed to be the case in this book. Here, in seeking to reconfigure Islamophobia, there is a collective need to refute attempts to negate and derogate Islamophobia as a real discriminatory phenomenon. This book and its approach to Islamophobia therefore are as necessary as they are important.

Dichotomous and Definitional Tensions

As previous chapters highlight, a substantial number of definitions of Islamophobia already exist. Whether in the political spaces or the scholarly equivalent, various definitions could be drawn upon to fulfil a whole host of needs, each of which would be wholly acceptable and without doubt 'fit for purpose'. While certain definitions may appeal to certain personal, professional or intellectual preferences, other definitions of Islamophobia may be more appropriate in certain specific contexts. This is neither problematic nor exceptional. Other discriminatory phenomena also have a similar multiplicity of definitions that have varying levels of appropriateness depending upon setting, context, function and more. What is exceptional about Islamophobia however is the oft-cited and unprecedented importance attributed to the 'need' to identify a sole definition that is consensually agreed by all and which functions in all settings and contexts without differentiation or divergence. That this 'need' does not exist as regards any other discriminatory phenomenon is clear evidence that those stating this 'need' are making demands of Islamophobia that are not made elsewhere. Some will argue that this is consequential of the dichotomous or definitional tensions referred to previously. As a reminder, these tensions emanate from the broad duality of definitions that are in circulation. In this way, the first problematically frames Islamophobia as a phobia through which the fear and dislike of the religion of Islam can be seen to have detrimental consequences and impacts for Muslims and their communities, while the second—more appropriately—frames Islamophobia as being akin to racism, specifically and directly targeting those who are or are perceived to be Muslim irrespective of religion, religiosity and so on. It is unquestionably the latter that the empirical data in Part II evidences and this book identifies with.

In spite of the overwhelming evidence to the contrary, conceptions and definitions of Islamophobia as being phobic continue to linger, thereby prompting and duly reinforcing literal interpretations and meanings about Islamophobia. At times, this would appear to be something of a quite deliberate endeavour, not least given the function such interpretations and meanings serve. Framing Islamophobia in this way, therefore, makes it extremely easy to argue that there is nothing discriminatory or hateful in being 'fearful of Islam'. To 'prove' this, attention is typically drawn to the atrocities committed by terrorists inspired by Islamist ideologies. Widely and routinely stated, an illustrative example is provided by Michael T. Flynn. Briefly serving as Donald Trump's National Security Advisor, Flynn claimed it was entirely rational to fear Islam (Gibbons-Neff, 2016). When challenged, Flynn, like others, deferred to the weakness and inappropriateness of the term used to define and 'describe'—rather than merely name—Islamophobia, claiming that it is that rather than their own skewed interpretation that is the problem. For them, the term can only ever be interpreted literally irrespective of the fact that they are in a minority. As the ongoing contestation can be seen to attribute undue importance to the 'need' to define Islamophobia, concurrent to this is a similar 'need' to understand and interpret Islamophobia literally. Some critics and detractors subsequently call for another term or phrase to be used, ignoring that it is their own interpretation that is problematic and inappropriate rather than the term itself. This argument found form in response to the APPG on British Muslims publishing its proposed working definition. As Mohammed Amin—Chair of the Conservative Muslim Forum—claimed, instead of trying to define Islamophobia, the APPG should 'abandon' the term before beginning its process of finding a definition (Amin, 2019). If a new term is used that better and more appropriately describes, why would there still be a 'need' to come up with a definition?

While this contestation shapes and determines much of the public and political debate about Islamophobia, the inconsistencies that are evident as regards Islamophobia and other similar discriminatory phenomena are roundly ignored. As with other discriminatory phenomena, Islamophobia is a term that merely names: it neither defines nor describes. The same is true of anti-Semitism and homophobia: both naming their respective phenomena without affording a basis for literal description or interpretation. In this way, while anti-Semitism is widely and unproblematically used to name the discrimination, bigotry, hate and violence expressed and manifested towards Jews and Jewish communities, it is a term that, if interpreted literally, would focus on 'Semites' not 'Jews'. Likewise, homophobia is a term widely and unproblematically used to name the discrimination, bigotry, hate and violence expressed towards those identifying as gay, lesbian, transgender and queer. If understood literally however, homophobia would only be appropriate if it was to refer to the fear of 'the same' (Greek) or of 'men' (Latin), neither of which reflect contemporary usage. Like anti-Semitism and homophobia however, Islamophobia is firmly established in national, regional and global lexicons as also the scholarly canon. Importantly, it is also the name preferred by victims of real and tangible manifestations and those lobbying for change. Substituting Islamophobia now would therefore be counter-intuitive and counter-productive. It would also do little as regards its contestation.

'Joined Up' or Disconnected and Disjointed?

Through considering the dichotomous and definitional tensions, it is possible to begin to make informed observations about the contestation of Islamophobia in the public and political spaces. Three observations in particular are especially pertinent. The first relates to how the contestation of Islamophobia shapes, informs and drives the public and political agenda. In addition to stating what terms are appropriate—or not as the case may be—so too does that same contestation necessitate key actions and activities: the 'need' to define being a case in point. Accordingly, the perceived inappropriateness of the term Islamophobia and the need to only interpret Islamophobia literally combine to divert attention away from the real and tangible manifestations of Islamophobia that are rather more pressing, dangerous and damaging. In this respect, it is telling how rare it is for the latter to feature in public or political discourses. The second is how Islamophobia is presented as exceptional, thereby justifying the wholly different demands placed on it when compared with other discriminatory phenomenon. This too serves a purpose: dismissing the very real similarities that exist between Islamophobia and other discriminatory phenomena while negating the view that Islamophobia is real and tangible. The result—of Islamophobia being exceptional and different—justifies the need for there to be a clear understanding of what exactly Islamophobia is and what exactly it is not. The third relates to how the 'need' for a definition plays out in the public and political spaces. Not only is this unnecessary but so too is it a response to an agenda driven by Islamophobia's contestation as also its critics and detractors.

Rather than the 'joined-up' approach identified as necessary in the opening chapter, what emerges is evidence of a substantive disconnect between Islamophobia as a publicly and politically contested concept and Islamophobia as a real discriminatory phenomenon. Two explanations emerge. The first is the lack of specificity attributed to Islamophobia when spoken about or referred to in the public and political spaces. Irrespective of Muslim or non-Muslim voices, the phenomenon is typically and routinely spoken about as an all-encompassing entity that lacks specificity or constraint. In this way, Islamophobia in the public and political spaces resonates with Hargreaves' (2015) concerns about how some scholarly studies aggregate under the term Islamophobia a vast array of different issues without explanation or evidence. Spanning a number of sociopolitical issues from representation in the media through to counter-terror policies, this broad-brush approach detracts as much as it diverts from the reality of Islamophobia both publicly and politically. The second is how public and political debates concerning Islamophobia err far more towards the religion of Islam than Muslims and their communities. To resolve this, a clear demarcation is needed between such things as discrimination, hate and violence that are targeted at individuals and communities and those notions that include defamation and blasphemy which target religions and beliefs. Doing so will go some way to countering arguments which suggest that Islamophobia is a mere means to deflect rightful criticism and condemnation of Islam and its teachings. Religions and religious teachings do not need to be afforded protection; people however—individuals and communities—sadly do.

Given the lack of joined-up thinking apparent, it is far from unsurprising that successive British Governments have failed to appropriately acknowledge and respond to Islamophobia in more than two decades. Instead, what has ensued has been a wholly disjointed approach. While various political mechanisms have been put in place and a handful of non-specific policy interventions have been introduced, none can be seen to have responded to the type of Islamophobia evidenced here. This is interesting given that evidence from both statutory (e.g. the Home Office and Metropolitan Police) and non-statutory (e.g. Tell MAMA) have repeatedly evidenced how Islamophobia—in the form of Islamophobically motivated hate crimes—is not only tangibly occurring but has also been increasing in recent years. Yet, none of the political mechanisms put in place have responded to this in any meaningful way nor have they sought to make meaningful links with those having responsibility for hate crime.

Affording this evidence—as also the concept of hate crime—scant attention or significance, the political mechanisms have instead focused on issues that fit and resonate with understandings of Islamophobia as an all-encompassing phenomenon. Knowing that political mechanisms and policy interventions are known to be most effective in curbing behaviours and activities rather than changing attitudes or opinions (Blakemore & Drake, 1996; Daniels and Macdonald, 2005), it is likely that responding to the rising levels of Islamophobically motivated hate crimes would have had a far greater impact than, say, focusing on media representation or organising countrywide iftars.

Islamophobia: Real and Tangible

While attention has been diverted away from the real and tangible in the public and political spaces, here the real and tangible are central to the book's focus, narrative and argument. Accordingly, Islamophobia is understood—and evidenced—as an unequivocally real and wholly contemporary discriminatory phenomenon. This book established and evidenced this in three ways. First, it affirms knowledge about Islamophobia drawn from the existing scholarly canon. Second, it develops certain aspects of that same existing knowledge, developing and subsequently building on that same existing canon. And third, it posits evidence from which new knowledge and thinking can be drawn in order to catalyse critical engagement and further investigation. As regards affirming existing knowledge, the ongoing role and function served by visual identifiers—equivalent to Carr's (2016) markers of Muslimness—continues to be widely apparent. In developing this however—and like the hijab and niqab—physical structures including mosques, beards and certain types of attire worn by Muslim men would also appear to function as markers of Muslimness. In this way, the evidence here suggests that all function symbolically: symbolic of the normative truths, those typically negative and problematic meanings and understandings routinely attributed to all Muslims without question or differentiation (Allen, 2010). Other aspects of existing knowledge that are duly affirmed include the preponderance of verbal abuse in the experience of Islamophobia, the catalytic function of terror-related incidents in prompting sharp increases of Islamophobia and the unquestioned assertion that Muslims 'do not belong', including the process of 'double-othering' where religious and racial markers are unproblematically co-joined.

As regards contributing new knowledge, evidence highlighted how real and tangible manifestations of Islamophobia can shift and transition, evident in the protean nature of the content of verbal abuse. Over time, the content of verbal abuse was shown to shift from insults relating to bin Laden through notions of Muslims being solider killers to associations and affiliations being made with ISIS most recently. Interesting too is the seeming correlation and shaping influence of geopolitics and the incidence and location of the UK and US-led military conflict. Reinforcing notions of Muslims as violent and prone to terrorism, the evidence also affirmed existing knowledge about Muslims being homogenised, essentialised and reduced without differentiation. The protean nature of the content of verbal abuse was also shown to respond to non-terror-related incidents: evident in the now widely prevalent insult, 'paedo'. Some correlation would also seem to exist between the prevalence of 'paedo' and the incidence of sexual exploitation incidents, the use of the phrase 'grooming gangs' in both media and political spaces and the adoption of such incidences by the radical right to mobilise support. Similar also is the shaping influence of political rhetoric, evidenced here by the incorporation of derogatory and mocking phrases made by Boris Johnson about Muslim women who wear face coverings. Not wanting to be drawn into adducing broad conclusions from relatively small samples however, these findings are preliminary and thereby require further investigation.

What is interesting is how the real and tangible Islamophobia that forms the core of this book is straightforwardly and without problem defined by the 'definition' posited previously: a tangible manifestation of Islamophobia can be understood as any malicious or violent act directed at Muslims (or those perceived to be Muslim) or any material entity associated with them where there exists evidence that the motivation, content or perpetrator focused on a perceived Muslim identity or other symbol of Muslims or Islam. Clear and unequivocal, it is however quite different from the working definition proposed by the APPG on British Muslims. The primary difference is specificity: evident in the definition above yet absent in the APPG alternative. As before, different definitions with different levels of specificity are necessary in different contexts and settings. Broad definitions of racism, for instance, require far less specificity than those that seek to define institutional racism specifically. While so, the APPG definition offers almost no specificity whatsoever. The Islamophobia that emerges therefore is—without doubt—an extremely broad one.

Defining Islamophobia

In joining up the various constituent arguments set out in this book, a narrative that focused on the public and political process of defining Islamophobia—in particular, the APPG on British Muslims—can be seen to have afforded a quite unique lens through which to structure as also investigate Islamophobia and its contestation. Drawing together the quite different—and at times, disparate and disjointed—parts of this book, this narrative helped to disentangle and deconstruct while also illustrate and elucidate the convergence and divergence apparent across the public, political and scholarly spaces. To do so, this narrative necessarily questioned what the APPG—and indeed others—was seeking to define, not least because numerous other similar and resonant definitions had already been established and duly circulated. In this respect, both the processes of definition as indeed the proposing of a definition seemed to offer nothing new nor any additional specificity. Add in that the definition offered little to narrow the focus, provide any greater meaningfulness or draw rightful attention to the real and tangible manifestations of Islamophobia and not only is its potential purpose further diminished but so too must the entire process be called into question. What then was the APPG—like others before and no doubt since—trying to define and, more importantly, achieve? Both questions resonate far more deeply however.

Here again, Islamophobia's contestation is pertinent in that it unquestionably shapes, informs and dictates public and political debate. Given that contestation's diversionary function—diverting attention away from the real and tangible—so the task of proposing a definition that is going to fulfil the needs of critics and detractors as also address that same contestation is always destined to fail: first, because it is unclear what exactly needs to be defined, and second, because no definition is going to be met with the widespread and unequivocal agreement and endorsement the parameters of contestation demand. That its critics and detractors allege that Islamophobia has the potential to limit free speech, detrimentally impact counter-extremism and counter-terrorism policies and afford protection to the religion of Islam to the extent that it will be unlawful to rightfully criticise does not necessarily mean that such allegations are factual or have ever been substantiated. In the context of a real and tangible Islamophobia evidenced here, none of these allegations find form let alone would appear to have any relevance whatsoever. That this is routinely overlooked is not only evidence that the focus of those seeking to propose a working definition are misdirected but so too that the realities of

Islamophobia have—and indeed remain—invisible in the public and political spaces. The lack of joined-up thinking therefore plays into the hands of and indeed strengthens those who seek to criticise, detract and dismiss Islamophobia out of hand.

Is a working definition of Islamophobia therefore necessary? From the evidence and analysis undertaken here, the answer is a clear and categorical no. Three arguments can be put forward in support of this. First, because public and political debates about Islamophobia and its contestation are indeterminably shaped and informed by the allegations made by its critics and detractors rather than by evidence or fact. Accordingly, no definition will ever satisfy their demands in that it is akin to trying to come up with a definition of racism that will convince racists that they themselves are racist. Trying to define Islamophobia in this way—one that appeases Islamophobes—is as nonsensical as it is unfathomable. The second is concomitant to Hargreaves' (2015) concerns about some scholarly studies. Accordingly, all those who participate in public and political debates about Islamophobia typically focus on an all-encompassing phenomenon that lacks meaningful specificity. Resultantly, all attempts to define are necessarily required to be as equally all-encompassing. Any definition that duly ensues therefore can only ever allude: never will it specify. Third, because Islamophobically motivated hate crimes—equivalent to the real and tangible manifestations of Islamophobia evidenced here—are successfully recorded and responded to without the need to have a definition in place beforehand. This not only refutes the 'need' for a definition but so too the allegation that Islamophobia has the potential to detrimentally impact police procedures.

Political Failure, Policy Impotence

As evidenced in the preceding two chapters, successive British Governments have categorically failed to acknowledge and respond to Islamophobia. As regards New Labour, it—like its critics and detractors—seemed unconvinced that Islamophobia was either specific or particularistic. Irrespective of whether that was due to a lack of understanding or because Islamophobia was seen to be a sub-manifestation of a more traditional racism, New Labour's response amounted to a handful of formal policy interventions that—inadvertently or otherwise—sought to address Islamophobia via the extension of protection afforded on the basis of religion and belief. Through informal—discursive—policy interventions, New Labour also began the process of causally aligning Islamophobia with counter-terrorism. Under successive Conservative-led Governments, that approach—initially at least—underwent significant change. Announcing that Islamophobia had passed the 'dinner table test', political mechanisms were quickly established that sought to investigate and respond. Within a short period of time however, the political will had dissipated, leaving in place mechanisms that served the purpose of providing the Conservatives with good PR at a time when greater scrutiny was highlighting how endemic Islamophobia seemed within its own rank and file. That its current leader—and now Prime Minister—has himself been far from exempt, it is now highly unlikely that any significant change will take place in the political spaces in the foreseeable future or that similar opportunities will be afforded.

Part of the problem as regards the political spaces has been the role and function played by those co-opted and tasked with 'representing' Muslim communities. As illustrated by the Cross-Government Working Group on Anti-Muslim Hate, the majority of those tasked with advocating and lobbying for change were shown to be far more interested in maintaining their seat at the Governmental table than anything else. Rather than hold successive Conservative-led Governments to account, they instead afforded credence and validation: credence and validation to Governments that failed to muster a single Islamophobia-specific political intervention in almost ten years. So too has the abject failure of Muslim groups and organisations to lobby as one been a factor in the political impasse that had led to the now readily apparent impotence in the public and political spaces. This is none more apparent than in the 2011 letter sent to Eric Pickles—then Secretary of State for Communities and Local Government and responsibility for the Working Group—by the newly formed Muslim Leadership Panel (MLP). Claiming that there were no existing groups or organisations that the Government could currently engage with to 'constructively converse' with the (singular) 'British Muslim community', it added that as 'leaders within their fields' its members were 'role models for the younger generation of British Muslims' (What Do They Know, 2012). Unfounded and unsubstantiated, the letter dismissed out of hand those groups and organisations that had for years been actively engaging with the Government on a whole range of different issues including Islamophobia. Maybe unsurprisingly, MLP members were subsequently appointed to and made up the majority of the Working Group's 'independent' membership. Those co-opted therefore need to reflect on themselves and their actions as much as they do those of the politicians and Governments.

Permission to Be Indolent

A number of different elements emerge from this narrative and comprise Islamophobia's contestation. These variously include: a lack of clarity about what Islamophobia is and what it is not; that the preferred term for naming the phenomenon (Islamophobia) is inappropriate; that the preferred term can only be understood and interpreted literally; that Islamophobia seeks to censor or close down all criticism of the religion of Islam (irrespective of whether that criticism is valid or not); that undue protection for the religion of Islam is being sought; that Islamophobia is part of the Islamification of the British and by extension, Western society and culture; that those advocating or lobbying for a political response to Islamophobia have a pernicious and underhanded agenda; that Islamophobia does not exist in any real or tangible ways and that Islamophobia is a mere fiction. Despite all being unfounded and unsubstantiated, it is rare that any are robustly refuted or that those doing the alleging are challenged or asked for evidence. Instead, the response has been to identify a definition that will allay each and every one of the previously stated allegations at the same time as appeasing the critics and detractors. Objectively viewed, it is a response that is as unrealistic as Islamophobia's contestation is unfounded. As a result, Islamophobia's contestation has to be seen as a mere smokescreen: one that functions to obfuscate Islamophobia as a real and tangible discriminatory phenomenon and which the evidence to support negated, derogated and made invisible.

It also serves another, more important function: the bestowing of permission to be indolent. To explain this, it is necessary to draw on Perry's (2002) theory relating to 'permission to hate'. According to her, the ongoing predication of divisive ideologies and ideas—including political discourses and mechanisms—that seek to demarcate 'us' from 'them' have the contemporarily function of constructing 'others' that are deemed indeterminably and insidiously oppositional, fearful and threatening. As she goes on however, this also contributes to the construction of public and political landscapes within which the hating of those same 'others' finds legitimacy and justification. Accordingly, these public and political landscapes bestow 'permission to hate'. While this theoretically explains why the number of real and tangible manifestations of Islamophobia has been increasing in recent years (Allen, 2018), a slight reworking offers a theoretical lens through which to 'join up' and better understand Islamophobia's contestation. As such, the ongoing predication of

Islamophobia's contestation—arguments and allegations that routinely negate and derogate any understanding of Islamophobia as a real discriminatory phenomenon—has contributed towards the construction of public and political landscapes where Islamophobia lacks credence and credibility. Not only does this undermine the attempt to afford importance to Islamophobia in the public and political spaces but so too does it bestow 'permission to be indolent' upon those in those same spaces. Resultantly, those in the public and political spaces are neither necessitated to act nor held to account when they do not. Indolence therefore is both normal and normative.

The process of defining Islamophobia once again affords a useful illustration through which to elucidate this. Beginning with the allegations and arguments of critics and detractors that Islamophobia is as confusing as it is complex, certain groups and organisations duly respond by identifying the 'need' to propose a definition that will simultaneously counter the allegations while also appeasing those alleging them. Proposing a definition that seeks to be all things to all people—including those whose agenda it is to detract and dismiss Islamophobia—the definition is established as the 'solution' to the 'problem'. Irrespective of whether the relevance or appropriateness of the definition that ensues—whether it is widely or variously endorsed—the critics and detractors who made the initial allegations once again dismiss it by regurgitating the exact same allegations. According to them, it is still no clearer what Islamophobia is and is not. Consequently, given the lack of a 'solution' let alone impetus created by a breakthrough, those in the political spaces do nothing. While certain groups and organisations—not necessarily the same ones referred to previously—begin the process once more by identifying the need for a definition, so permission to be indolent as regards Islamophobia is duly bestowed. With no constituency holding anyone to account—not even those tasked with doing so on behalf of Muslim communities—political indolence can be dismissed without explanation or regard at least that is until a 'solution' to the 'problem' is found.

Reconfiguring Islamophobia: What Next?

In the opening chapter, a series of rhetorical questions were posited that now require a response. The first questioned whether the 'problem' lies with Islamophobia being more difficult to define than other discriminatory phenomena. The answer is unequivocally no. Neither the process nor the actual defining of Islamophobia is any more difficult or problematic than it is with other discriminatory phenomena. What is different as regards Islamophobia is the importance attributed to the 'need' to define, the underlying reasons for doing so and the diverting function the process clearly serves. The second asked whether the APPG definition was the 'problem'. The answer again is no. Like other definitions, the APPG is quite unproblematic albeit with the caveat that it embodies breadth in preference of specificity. Accordingly—and in answering the third question—this is because the APPG gave far too much credence to the unsubstantiated allegations of Islamophobia's critics and detractors. The fourth questioned whether the process and subsequent definition of Islamophobia overlooked or at least negated the reality of Islamophobia being a real and tangible discriminatory phenomenon. As evidenced here, Islamophobia's realities are not only overlooked but are completely invisibilised in the public and political spaces. The fifth questioned the extent to which the process of definition functioned as a smokescreen. Undoubtedly so. Both the process and subsequent 'need' to define Islamophobia has been deliberately and routinely deployed: first, to divert attention away from the real and tangible manifestations of Islamophobia; and second, to divert attention away from the impotence and indolence of successive governments.

In seeking to reconfigure Islamophobia, this book has radically rethought, reanalysed and reconstructed not only Islamophobia as a discriminatory phenomenon in the public, political and scholarly spaces but so too the contestation associated with it over the past two decades. In addition, this book has evidenced how Islamophobia in its broadest conception is a highly political and politicised phenomenon. So too is its contestation. As stated at the outset, this book did not seek to put forward a 'solution' or to merely offer a new definition of Islamophobia. Instead, it sought to improve understanding about Islamophobia through the presentation of new evidence relating to the experience of real and tangible manifestations while simultaneously investigating political approaches to both Islamophobia and its contestation. In doing so, this book has reframed and reconfigured existing knowledge and understanding about Islamophobia at the same time as contributing new evidence, understanding and knowledge. As a phenomenon that has—to date at least—been understood and approached in largely disjointed ways, this book has also worked towards 'joining up' the different spaces within which Islamophobia manifests and can be seen to have meaning. It began this process by 'joining up' Islamophobia as a real and tangible discriminatory phenomenon with Islamophobia that is rather more all-encompassing and, by consequence, politically problematic.

This was meaningfully and accessibly illustrated through creating a narrative around the need and subsequent process of defining Islamophobia in the public and political spaces.

As regards 'what next?', this book posits three possible outcomes. The first is to dismiss out of hand the evidence, arguments and narratives set out in this book. This might take the form of some alleging the author is himself part of the pernicious agenda critics and detractors infer. Some might do so to further divert attention away from the evidence that 'proves' Islamophobia is a real discriminatory phenomenon. Others might rely on political or personal reasons given the author's public denouncement of the Cross-Government Working Group on Anti-Muslim Hate and its members, for being an outspoken critic of different—and indeed current—British Governments, or having rightfully called out certain Muslim groups and organisations. The second is to ignore this book and continue doing exactly the same things that have to date had no impact whatsoever. While absurd, continuing to do exactly the same is what the current Conservative Government has already chosen to do. During the final editing of this book, the Ministry for Housing, Communities and Local Government—formerly the Department for Communities and Local Government—announced the appointment of an independent adviser who will lead work on identifying a definition of Islamophobia (Ministry for Housing, Communities and Local Government, 2019). That independent adviser has been named as Imam Qari Asim, a member of the Cross-Government's Working Group on Anti-Muslim Hate since its establishment in 2012. While further permission to be indolent will no doubt ensue, it is quite staggering that the process has been started once again. That it is fronted by someone who has been integral to the political mechanisms that have abjectly failed is unbelievable.

The third response is that the book, the evidence set out in it and the conclusions drawn catalyse (radical?) change across the scholarly, public and political spaces. As regards the scholarly, it is hoped that the new evidence, new thinking and new knowledge presented will be critically engaged with in order to challenge others to rethink and reconfigure their own conceptions and understandings about Islamophobia. It is also hoped that the new findings preliminarily evidenced will provide a foundation upon which others engage and investigate more fully: to build on and develop those third wave studies referred to previously while also forging new frontiers in scholarly inquiry that seek to investigate institutional Islamophobia among others. As regards the public spaces, it is hoped that this book will challenge the ongoing albeit largely unsubstantiated contestation. Whether through highlighting the paucity of evidence underpinning the unfounded claims that are regularly and routinely put forward by Islamophobia's critics and detractors or through highlighting the need to shift the focus away from an all-encompassing and rather more problematic Islamophobia, the need to focus on Islamophobia as a real discriminatory phenomenon is long overdue. So too the political where attention and focus has been conveniently—and equally, for far too long—diverted away from that same real Islamophobia. Through highlighting the failure of successive British Governments—and politics more broadly—to respond to rising levels of Islamophobic hate crime despite having the data to 'prove' this, it is hoped that this book will catalyse others to hold those with political power to account both in terms of their own actions and also the need to design and deliver appropriate and meaningful political mechanisms and policy interventions. No longer can those in the political spaces be afforded permission to be indolent.

References

Allen, C. (2010). *Islamophobia*. Farnham: Ashgate.

Allen, C. (2018). Hasskriminalität in Großbritannien. *Wissen schafft Demokratie, 4*, 84–93.

Amin, M. (2019). Mohammed Amin: It is time to abandon the word "Islamophobia". *Conservative Home*. Retrieved from https://www.conservativehome.com/platform/2019/02/mohammed-amin-it-is-time-to-abandon-the-word-islamophobia.html

Blakemore, K., & Drake, R. F. (1996). *Understanding equal opportunity policies*. New York: Prentice Hall Professional Technical Reference.

Carr, J. (2016). *Experiences of Islamophobia: Living with racism in the neoliberal era*. Abingdon: Routledge.

Daniels, K., & Macdonald, L. A. C. (2005). *Equality, diversity and discrimination*. London: Chartered Institute of Personnel and Development.

Gibbons-Neff, T. (2016). 'Fear of Muslims is rational': What Trump's new national security adviser has said online. *Washington Post*. Retrieved from https://www.washingtonpost.com/news/checkpoint/wp/2016/11/18/trumps-new-national-security-adviser-has-said-some-incendiary-things-on-the-internet/?noredirect=on

Hargreaves, J. (2015). Half a story? Missing perspectives in the criminological accounts of British Muslim communities, crime and the criminal justice system. *British Journal of Criminology, 55*(1), 19–38.

Ministry for Housing, Communities and Local Government. (2019). Independent expert appointed to tackle Islamophobia. *Ministry for Housing, Communities and Local Government*. Retrieved from https://www.wired-gov.net/wg/news.nsf/articles/Independent+expert+appointed+to+tackle+Islamophobia+24072019081000?open

Perry, B. (2002). *In the name of hate: Understanding hate crimes*. London: Routledge.

What Do They Know. (2012). Remit/membership of the Muslim Leadership Panel. *What Do They Know*. Retrieved from https://www.whatdotheyknow.com/request/136128/response/336750/attach/html/4/2011%2011%2014%20MLPmembers1.tif.html

References

Abu-Lughod, L. (2002). Do Muslim women really need saving? Anthropological reflections on cultural relativism and its others. *American Anthropologist, 104*(3), 783–790.

Afridi, A. (2015). *From benign neglect to Citizen Khan: 30 years of equalities practice in Birmingham*. Birmingham: BRAP.

Afshar, H. (1994). *Muslim women in West Yorkshire*. London: Taylor and Francis.

Afshar, H. (2008). Can I see your hair? Choice, agency and attitudes: The dilemma of faith and feminism for Muslim women who cover. *Ethnic and Racial Studies, 31*(2), 411–427.

Afshar, H., Aitken, R., & Franks, M. (2005). Feminisms, Islamophobia and identities. *Political Studies, 53*(2), 262–283.

Ali, Y. (1992). Muslim women and the politics of ethnicity and culture in Northern England. In S. Gita & N. Yuval-Davis (Eds.), *Refusing holy orders: Women and fundamentalism in Britain* (pp. 101–123). London: Sage.

All Party Parliamentary Group on British Muslims. (2017). *A very merry Muslim Christmas*. London: All Party Parliamentary Group on British Muslims.

All Party Parliamentary Group on British Muslims. (2018a). *Faith as the fourth emergency service: British Muslim charitable contributions to the UK*. London: All Party Parliamentary Group on British Muslims.

All Party Parliamentary Group on British Muslims. (2018b). *Islamophobia defined: The inquiry into a working definition of Islamophobia*. London: All Party Parliamentary Group on British Muslims.

Allen, C. (2005). From race to religion: The new face of discrimination. In T. Abbas (Ed.), *Muslim Britain: Communities under pressure*. London, UK: Zed Books.

Allen, C. (2010a). *Islamophobia*. Farnham: Ashgate.

C. Allen, *Reconfiguring Islamophobia*, Palgrave Hate Studies,
https://doi.org/10.1007/978-3-030-33047-7

Allen, C. (2010b). Fear and loathing: The political discourse in relation to Muslims and Islam in the British contemporary setting. *Politics and Religion Journal, 4*(2), 221–236.

Allen, C. (2010c). Islamophobia: From KISS to RIP. In S. Sayyid & A. Vakil (Eds.), *Thinking through Islamophobia: Global perspectives* (pp. 51–64). London: Hurst & Co.

Allen, C. (2011a). *A momentous occasion: A report on the All Party Parliamentary Group on Islamophobia and its secretariat.* London: All Party Parliamentary Group on Islamophobia.

Allen, C. (2011b). 'We don't do God': A critical retrospective of New Labour's approaches to 'religion or belief' and 'faith'. *Culture and Religion, 12*(3), 259–275.

Allen, C. (2013a). Between critical and uncritical understandings: A case study analyzing the claims of Islamophobia made in the context of the proposed "super-mosque" in Dudley, England. *Societies, 3*(2), 186–203.

Allen, C. (2013b). Passing the dinner table test: Retrospective and prospective approaches to tackling Islamophobia in Britain. *SAGE Open, 3*(2).

Allen, C. (2014a). Exploring the impact of Islamophobia on visible Muslim women victims: A British case study. *Journal of Muslims in Europe, 3*(2), 137–159.

Allen, C. (2014b). Operation Trojan Horse: How a hoax problematised Muslims and Islam. *Discover Society.* Retrieved from https://discoversociety.org/2014/07/01/operation-trojan-horse-how-a-hoax-problematised-muslims-and-islam/

Allen, C. (2014c). Why I Quit the Government's Anti-Muslim Hatred Working Group. *Huffington Post.* Retrieved from https://www.huffingtonpost.co.uk/dr-chris-allen/anti-muslim-hatred-working-group_b_6064866.html

Allen, C. (2015). 'People hate you because of the way you dress': Understanding the invisible experiences of veiled British Muslim women victims of Islamophobia. *International Review of Victimology, 21*(3), 287–301.

Allen, C. (2016). By banning the burkini, the French are blaming Muslims. *HuffPost.* Retrieved from https://www.huffingtonpost.co.uk/dr-chris-allen/burkini-ban-france_b_11535276.html

Allen, C. (2017a). Islamophobia. In D. Thomas (Ed.), *The Routledge handbook on Christian-Muslim relations* (pp. 376–383). London: Routledge.

Allen, C. (2017b). Islamophobia and the problematization of mosques: A critical exploration of hate crimes and the symbolic function of "old" and "new" mosques in the United Kingdom. *Journal of Muslim Minority Affairs, 37*(3), 294–308.

Allen, C. (2017c). Political approaches to tackling Islamophobia: An 'insider/outsider' analysis of the British Coalition Government's approach between 2010–15. *Social Sciences, 6*(3), 77.

Allen, C. (2018a). Hasskriminalität in Großbritannien. *Wissen schafft Demokratie, 4*, 84–93.

Allen, C. (2018b). A Summer of Islamophobia: Considering the lessons learned. *Medium*. Retrieved from https://medium.com/@mail.chrisallen/a-summer-of-islamophobia-considerations-of-the-lessons-learned-9d7b85b05014

Allen, C. (2018c). It was always Islamophobia, never a 'gaffe': How attention is now being deflected away from Johnson. *Medium*. Retrieved from https://medium.com/@mail.chrisallen/it-was-always-islamophobia-never-a-gaffe-how-attention-is-now-being-deflected-away-from-johnson-c2f1ffc7d8d6

Allen, C. (2019). *Islamophobia defined*. London: Religion Media Centre.

Allen, C., Isakjee, A., & Ögtem-Young, Ö. (2013). *Maybe we are hated: The experience and impact of anti-Muslim hate on British Muslim women*. Birmingham: University of Birmingham.

Allen, C., & Nielsen, J. S. (2002). *Summary report on Islamophobia in the EU after 11 September 2001*. Vienna: EUMC.

Allievi, S. (2009). *Conflicts over mosques in Europe: Policy issues and trends*. London: Alliance Publishing Trust.

Amin, M. (2019). Mohammed Amin: It is time to abandon the word "Islamophobia". *Conservative Home*. Retrieved from https://www.conservativehome.com/platform/2019/02/mohammed-amin-it-is-time-to-abandon-the-word-islamophobia.html

Amir-Moazami, S. (2011). Dialogue as a Governmental technique: Managing gendered Islam in Germany. *Feminist Review, 98*(1), 9–27.

Anwar, M., & Bakhsh, Q. (2003). *British Muslims and state policies*. Coventry, UK: Centre for Research in Ethnic Relations.

Archer, L. (2001). 'Muslim brothers, black lads, traditional Asians': British Muslim young men's constructions of race, religion and masculinity. *Feminism & Psychology, 11*(1), 79–105.

Aslam, M. (2012). *Gender-based explosions: The nexus between Muslim masculinities, jihadist Islamism and terrorism*. UNU Press.

Awan, I. (2017). The non-Muslims experiencing Islamophobic attacks. *New Statesman*. Retrieved from https://www.newstatesman.com/politics/staggers/2017/10/non-muslims-experiencing-islamophobic-attacks

Awan, I., & Zempi, I. (2016). The affinity between online and offline anti-Muslim hate crime: Dynamics and impacts. *Aggression and Violent Behavior, 27*, 1–8.

BBC News. (2002, August 6). Guard dumped pigs' heads at mosque. *BBC England*. Retrieved from http://news.bbc.co.uk/1/hi/england/2176553.stm

BBC News. (2007). UK teacher jailed over teddy row. *BBC News*. Retrieved from http://news.bbc.co.uk/1/hi/world/africa/7119399.stm

BBC News. (2009). Tory Muslim peer pelted with eggs. *BBC News*. Retrieved from http://news.bbc.co.uk/1/hi/england/beds/bucks/herts/8387110.stm

BBC News. (2019). US House condemns Trump attacks on congresswomen as racist. *BBC News*. Retrieved from https://www.bbc.co.uk/news/world-us-canada-49011843

Bhavani, R., Mirza, H. S., & Meetoo, V. (2005). *Tackling the roots of racism: Lessons for success*. Bristol: Policy Press.

Bingham, J. (2013). Banning veil would be like outlawing miniskirts, says Baroness Warsi. *Telegraph*. Retrieved from http://www.telegraph.co.uk/news/religion/10421608/Banning-veil-would-be-like-outlawing-miniskirts-says-Baroness-Warsi.html

Blakemore, K., & Drake, R. F. (1996). *Understanding equal opportunity policies*. New York: Prentice Hall Professional Technical Reference.

Bogacki, M., de Ruiter, J. J., & Sèze, R. (2019). Defining Islamophobia and its socio-political applications in the light of the Charlie Hebdo attacks in Paris. *Rosenberg Quarterly*. Retrieved from http://rozenbergquarterly.com/defining-islamophobia-and-its-socio-political-applications-in-the-light-of-the-charlie-hebdo-attacks-in-paris-2/

Bourke, B. (2014). Positionality: Reflecting on the research process. *The Qualitative Report, 19*(33), 1–9.

Bowen, J. R. (2007). Why the French don't like headscarves: Islam, the state, and public space. *European Review, 15*(3), 397–400.

Bracke, S. (2011). Subjects of debate: Secular and sexual exceptionalism, and Muslim women in the Netherlands. *Feminist Review, 98*(1), 28–46.

Bridge Institute. (2017). *A new era in American politics: The Trump administration and mainstream Islamophobia*. Georgetown: Georgetown University.

Brown, K. (2002). Realising Muslim women's rights: The role of Islamic identity among British Muslim women. *Women's Studies International Forum, 29*(4), 417–430.

Brown, K. (2008). The promise and perils of women's participation in UK mosques: The impact of securitisation agendas on identity, gender and community. *British Journal Politics and International Relations, 10*(3), 472–491.

Bruce, S. (1996). *Religion in the modern world: From cathedrals to cults*. Oxford: Oxford University Press.

Carr, J. (2016). *Experiences of Islamophobia: Living with racism in the neoliberal era*. Abingdon: Routledge.

Cesari, J. (2005). Mosques in French cities: Towards the end of a conflict? *Journal of Ethnic and Migration Studies, 31*(6), 1025–1043.

Chakraborti, N., & Zempi, I. (2012). The veil under attack: Gendered dimensions of Islamophobic victimization. *International Review of Victimology, 18*(3), 269–284.

Clarke, S. (2003). *Social theory, psychoanalysis and racism*. Basingstoke: Palgrave Macmillan.

Cohen, D. J., & Crabtree, B. F. (2008). Evaluative criteria for qualitative research in health care; Controversies and recommendations. *Annals of Family Medicine, 6*(4), 331–339.

Commission on British Muslims and Islamophobia. (1997). *Islamophobia: A challenge for us all.* London: Runnymede Trust.

Cooper, D. (2004). *Challenging diversity: Rethinking equality and the value of difference.* Cambridge: Cambridge University Press.

Council of Europe. (2005). *Islamophobia and its consequences on young people.* Vienna: COE.

Dagistanli, S., & Grewal, K. (2012). Perverse Muslim masculinities in contemporary orientalist discourse: The vagaries of Muslim immigration in the West. In *Global Islamophobia: Muslims and moral panic in the West* (pp. 119–142). Surrey: Ashgate Publishing Ltd.

Daniel, N. (2000). *Islam and the West: The making of an image.* Oxford: Oneworld.

Daniels, K., & Macdonald, L. A. C. (2005). *Equality, diversity and discrimination.* London: Chartered Institute of Personnel and Development.

Davie, G. (1994). *Religion in Britain since 1945: Believing without belonging.* Oxford, UK: Basil Blackwell.

De Payer, R. (2018). Revealed: Anti-Muslim hate crimes in London soared by 40% in a year. *The London Standard.* Retrieved from https://www.standard.co.uk/news/crime/revealed-antimuslim-hate-crimes-in-london-soared-by-40-in-a-year-a3775751.html

Dearden, L. (2018). 'Letterbox' insults against Muslim women spike in wake of Boris Johnson comments. *The Independent.* Retrieved from https://www.independent.co.uk/news/uk/home-news/boris-johnson-burqa-muslim-women-veil-attacks-islamophobia-letterboxes-rise-a8488651.html

Denham, J. (2001, September 29). Keynote address. *Exploring Islamophobia Conference.* University of Westminster, London, UK.

Dodd, V. (2019). Police chiefs in row over definition of Islamophobia. *The Guardian.* Retrieved from https://www.theguardian.com/news/2019/may/15/police-chiefs-in-row-over-definition-of-islamophobia

Driessen, G., & Merry, M. S. (2006). Islamic schools in the Netherlands: Expansion or marginalization? *Interchange, 37*(3), 201–223.

Dwyer, C. (1999a). Contradictions of community: Questions of identity for young British Muslim women. *Environment and Planning, 31*(1), 53–68.

Dwyer, C. (1999b). Veiled Meanings: Young British Muslim women and the negotiation of differences. *Gender, Place and Culture: A Journal of Feminist Geography, 6*(1), 5–26.

Dwyer, C. (2000). Negotiating diasporic identities: Young British south Asian Muslim women. *Women's Studies International Forum, 23*(4), 475–486.

Dwyer, C., & Meyer, A. (1995). The institutionalisation of Islam in the Netherlands and in the UK: The case of Islamic schools. *Journal of Ethnic and Migration Studies, 21*(1), 37–54.

Dwyer, C., Shah, B., & Sanghera, G. (2008). 'From cricket lover to terror suspect' – Challenging representations of young British Muslim men. *Gender, Place & Culture, 15*(2), 117–136.

Embury-Dennis, T. (2019). Trump tells fake story about US general slaughtering 49 Muslims using bullets dipped in pig's blood, in resurfaced video. *The Independent*. Retrieved from https://www.independent.co.uk/news/world/americas/us-politics/trump-muslims-general-pershing-pigs-blood-video-a8829676.html

Esposito, J. (1994). *The Islamic threat: Myth or reality?* Oxford: Oxford University Press.

European Monitoring Centre on Racism and Xenophobia. (2007). *Muslims in the European Union: Discrimination and Islamophobia*. Vienna, Austria.

Ewing, K. P. (2008). *Stolen honor: Stigmatizing Muslim men in Berlin*. Stanford University Press.

Fernando, M. (2009). Exceptional citizens: Secular Muslim women and the politics of difference in France. *Social Anthropology, 17*(4), 379–392.

Franks, M. (2000). Crossing the borders of whiteness? White Muslim women who wear the hijab in Britain today. *Ethnic and Racial Studies, 23*(5), 917–929.

Fuller, G. (2018). *A sense of siege: The geopolitics of Islam and the West*. London: Routledge.

Fundamental Rights Agency. (2009). *Data in focus report: Muslims*. Vienna: European Union Agency for Fundamental Rights.

Gale, R. (2005). Representing the city: Mosques and the planning process in Birmingham. *Journal of Ethnic and Migration Studies, 31*(6), 1161–1179.

Gibbons-Neff, T. (2016). 'Fear of Muslims is rational': What Trump's new national security adviser has said online. *Washington Post*. Retrieved from https://www.washingtonpost.com/news/checkpoint/wp/2016/11/18/trumps-new-national-security-adviser-has-said-some-incendiary-things-on-the-internet/?noredirect=on

Gilliat-Ray, S. (2004). The trouble with 'inclusion': A case study of the faith zone at the Millennium Dome. *The Sociological Review, 52*(4), 459–477.

Greater London Authority. (2007). *The search for common ground: Muslims, non-Muslims and the UK media*. London: Greater London Authority.

Gündüz, Z. Y. (2010). The European Union at 50—Xenophobia, Islamophobia and the rise of the radical right. *Journal of Muslim Minority Affairs, 30*(1), 35–47.

Hall, S. (1979). *Policing the crisis: Mugging, the state, and law and order*. New York: Palgrave Macmillan.

Hall, S., Critcher, C., Jefferson, T., Clarke, J., & Roberts, B. (1978). *Policing the crisis: Mugging, the state and law and order*. London: Macmillan.

Hall, S., & O'Shea, A. (2013). Common-sense neoliberalism. *Soundings, 55*(55), 9–25.

Halliday, F. (1999). *Islam and the myth of confrontation: Religion and politics in the Middle East.* London: I.B. Tauris.
Hannes, K. (2011). Critical appraisal of qualitative research. In J. Noyes, A. Booth, K. Hannes, A. Harden, J. Harris, S. Lewin, & C. Lockwood (Eds.), *Supplementary guidance for inclusion of qualitative research in Cochrane systematic reviews of interventions.* Cochrane Collaboration Qualitative Methods Group. Retrieved from http://cqrmg.cochrane.org/supplemental-handbook-guidance
Hargreaves, J. (2015). Half a story? Missing perspectives in the criminological accounts of British Muslim communities, crime and the criminal justice system. *British Journal of Criminology, 55*(1), 19–38.
Harris, M., Halfpenny, P., & Rochester, C. (2003). A social policy role for faith-based organisations? Lessons from the UK Jewish voluntary sector. *Journal of Social Policy, 32*, 93–112.
Haw, K. (2010). Being, becoming and belonging: Young Muslim women in contemporary Britain. *Journal of Intercultural Studies, 31*(4), 345–361.
Heidegger, M. (2002). *On time and being.* Chicago: University of Chicago Press.
Helbling, M. (2010). Islamophobia in Switzerland: A new phenomenon or a new name for xenophobia? In S. Hug & H. Kriesi (Eds.), *Value change in Switzerland* (pp. 65–80). Lanham: Lexington Books.
HM Government. (2017). *Action against hate, the UK government's plan for tackling hate crime – 'Two years on'.* London: HMSO.
Hödl, K. (2010). Islamophobia in Austria: The recent emergence of anti-Muslim sentiments in the country. *Journal of Muslim Minority Affairs, 30*(4), 443–456.
Hopkins, P. (2007). Global events, national politics, local lives: Young Muslim men in Scotland. *Environment and Planning A, 39*(5), 1119–1133.
Hopkins, P. E. (2006). Youthful Muslim masculinities: Gender and generational relations. *Transactions of the Institute of British Geographers, 31*(3), 337–352.
Huisman, K. (2008). Does this mean you're not going to come visit me anymore? An inquiry into an ethics of reciprocity and positionality in feminist ethnographic research. *Sociological Inquiry, 78*, 372–396.
Hussain, D. (2004). The impact of 9/11 on British Muslim identity. In R. Geaves (Ed.), *Islam and the West: A post September 11th perspective* (pp. 115–129). London: Ashgate.
Jackson, L. B. (2018). *Islamophobia in Britain: The making of a Muslim enemy.* Cham: Palgrave Macmillan.
Jaschok, M., & Shui, S. J. (2013). *The history of women's mosques in Chinese Islam.* Routledge.
Jenkins, R., & Solomos, J. (1989). Racism, equal opportunity and public policy. In R. Jenkins & J. Solomos (Eds.), *Racism and equal opportunity policies in the 1980s* (pp. 3–29). Cambridge, UK: Cambridge University Press.

Johnson, B. (2018). Denmark has got it wrong. Yes, the burka is oppressive and ridiculous – But that's still no reason to ban it. *Telegraph*. Retrieved from https://www.telegraph.co.uk/news/2018/08/05/denmark-has-got-wrong-yes-burka-oppressive-ridiculous-still/

Jones, J. (2016). There have been more than 300 reported hate incidents since election day. *Think Progress*. Retrieved from https://thinkprogress.org/300-hate-incidents-since-election-day-bf9fd91edbd6/#.43wykakta

Jones, S. H., O'Toole, T., DeHanas, D. N., Modood, T., & Meer, N. (2015). A 'system of self-appointed leaders'? Examining modes of Muslim representation in governance in Britain. *The British Journal of Politics and International Relations, 17*(2), 207–223.

Jouili, J. S., & Amir-Moazami, S. (2006). Knowledge, empowerment and religious authority among pious Muslim women in France and Germany. *The Muslim World, 96*(4), 617–642.

Kalra, V. S. (2009). Between emasculation and hypermasculinity: Theorizing British South Asian masculinities. *South Asian Popular Culture, 7*(2), 113–125.

Kavanagh, T. (2019). Hidden women. *The Sun*. Retrieved from https://www.thesun.co.uk/news/opinion/9059873/tories-dead-boris-johnson-survive/

Kayaoglu, A., & Kaya, A. (2012). *A quantitative analysis of Islamophobia in EU-15*. Leuven: University of Leuven.

Klaus, E., & Kassel, S. (2005). The veil as a means of legitimisation: An analysis of the interconnectedness of gender, media and war. *Journalism, 6*(3), 335–355.

Klug, B. (2012). Islamophobia: A concept comes of age. *Ethnicities, 12*(5), 665–681.

Knott, K., & Khokher, S. (1993). Religious and ethnic identity among young Muslim women in Bradford. *Journal of Ethnic and Migration Studies, 19*(4), 593–610.

Kühnel, S., & Leibold, J. (2007). Islamophobie in der deutschen Bevölkerung: ein neues Phänomen oder nur ein neuer Namen? Ergebnisse von Bevölkerungsumfragen zur Gruppenbezogenen Menschenfeindlichkeit 2003 bis 2005. In M. Wohlrab-Sahr & L. Tezcan (Eds.), *Konfliktfeld Islam in Europa* (pp. 135–154). Baden-Baden: Nomos.

Kumar, D. (2012). *Islamophobia and the politics of empire*. New York: Haymarket Books.

Landman, N., & Wessels, W. (2005). The visibility of mosques in Dutch towns. *Journal of Ethnic and Migration Studies, 31*(6), 1125–1140.

Macey, M. (1999). Religion, male violence, and the control of women: Pakistani Muslim men in Bradford, UK. *Gender & Development, 7*(1), 48–55.

Macey, M. (2007). *Islamic political radicalism in Britain: Muslim men in Bradford*. In T. Abbas (Ed.), *Islamic political radicalism: A European comparative perspective* (pp. 160–172). Edinburgh: Edinburgh University Press.

Malik, K. (2005). *Transcript of Kenan Malik's film "Are Muslims Hated?"* Retrieved December 12, 2016, from http://www.kenanmalik.com/tv/c4_islamophobia.html

Marshall, M. N. (1996). Sampling for qualitative research. *Family Practice, 13*(6), 522–526.

McGinty, A. M. (2007). Formation of alternative femininities through Islam: Feminist approaches among Muslim converts in Sweden. *Women's Studies International Forum, 30*(6), 474–485.

McLoughlin, S. (2003). Islam, citizenship and civil society: "New" Muslim leaderships in the UK. In J. Cesari (Ed.), *European Muslims and the secular state in a comparative perspective* (pp. 100–124). Paris, France: Network on Comparative Research on Islam and Muslims in Europe.

McLoughlin, S. (2005). Mosques and the public space: Conflict and cooperation in Bradford. *Journal of Ethnic and Migration Studies, 31*(6), 1045–1066.

McLoughlin, S. (2010). From race to faith relations, the local to the national level: The state and Muslim organisations in Britain. In A. Kreienbrink & M. Bodenstein (Eds.), *Muslim organisations and the state: European perspectives* (pp. 123–149). Nürnberg, Bavaria, Germany: Bundesamt für Migration und Flüchtlinge.

Merriam, S. B., Johnson-Bailey, J., Lee, M. Y., Kee, Y., Ntseane, G., & Muhamad, M. (2001). Power and positionality: Negotiating insider/outsider status within and across cultures. *International Journal of Lifelong Education, 20*(5), 405–416.

Miles, R. (1989). *Racism*. London: Routledge.

Miles, R., & Brown, M. (2003). *Racism*. London: Psychology Press.

Milner IV, H. R. (2007). Race, culture, and researcher positionality: Working through dangers seen, unseen, and unforeseen. *Educational Researcher, 36*(7), 388–400.

Milton-Edwards, B. (2002). Researching the radical: The quest for a new perspective. In H. Donnan (Ed.), *Interpreting Islam* (pp. 32–50). London: Sage.

Ministry for Housing, Communities and Local Government. (2019). Independent expert appointed to tackle Islamophobia. *Ministry for Housing, Communities and Local Government*. Retrieved from https://www.wired-gov.net/wg/news.nsf/articles/Independent+expert+appointed+to+tackle+Islamophobia+24072019081000?open

Moosavi, L. (2012). British Muslim converts performing 'authentic Muslimness'. *Performing Islam, 1*(1), 103–128.

Moosavi, L. (2014a). The racialization of Muslim converts in Britain and their experiences of Islamophobia. *Critical Sociology, 41*(1), 41–56.

Moosavi, L. (2014b). Orientalism at home: Islamophobia in the representations of Islam and Muslims by the New Labour government. *Ethnicities, 14*(3), 1–23.

Morse, J. M. (1999). Qualitative generalizability. *Qualitative Health Research, 9*(1), 5–6.

Murray, D. (2018). The Islamophobia 'problem'. *The Spectator*. Retrieved from https://blogs.spectator.co.uk/2018/11/the-islamophobia-problem/

National Centre for Social Research. (2010). *British social attitudes survey 2010* (26th ed.). London, UK: NatCen.

Nicks, G. (2010). Conservative chairwoman: Don't ban burka. *Daily Star*. Retrieved from http://www.dailystar.co.uk/news/latest-news/147549/Conservative-chairwoman-Don-t-ban-burka

Nussbaum, M. C. (2012). *the new religious intolerance: Overcoming the politics of fear in an anxious age*. Cambridge, MA: Belknap Press of Harvard University Press.

O'Neill, A. (2017). *Hate crime, England and Wales, 2016/17: Statistical bulletin 17/17*. London: Home Office.

Oliver-Dee, S. (2009). *Religion and identity: Divided loyalties?* London, UK: Theos.

Organisation of Islamic Cooperation. (2008). *1st OIC observatory report on Islamophobia*. Kampala, Uganda: OIC.

Ozalt, M. (2017). Islamophobia is still raising its ugly head in Australia. *The Conversation*. Retrieved from https://theconversation.com/islamophobia-is-still-raising-its-ugly-head-in-australia-80682

Perry, B. (2002). *In the name of hate: Understanding hate crimes*. London: Routledge.

Phillips, M. (2018). Islamophobia is a fiction to shut down debate. *The Times*. Retrieved from https://www.thetimes.co.uk/article/islamophobia-is-a-fiction-to-shut-down-debate-wwtzggnc7

Polit, D. F., & Beck, C. T. (2010). Generalization in quantitative and qualitative research: Myths and strategies. *International Journal of Nursing Studies, 47*(11), 1451–1458.

Predelli, L. N. (2004). Interpreting gender in Islam: A case study of immigrant Muslim women in Oslo, Norway. *Gender & Society, 18*(4), 473–493.

Rashid, H. M., & Muhammad, Z. (1992). The Sister Clara Muhammad schools: Pioneers in the development of Islamic education in America. *The Journal of Negro Education, 61*(2), 178–185.

Razack, S. H. (2004). Imperilled Muslim women, dangerous Muslim men and civilised Europeans: Legal and social responses to forced marriages. *Feminist Legal Studies, 12*(2), 129–174.

Readings, G., Brandon, J., & Phelps, R. (2011). *Islamism and language: How using the wrong words reinforces Islamist narratives*. London: Quilliam Foundation.

Riddell, S., & Watson, N. (2011). Equality and human rights in Britain: Principles and challenges. *Social Policy and Society, 10*, 193–203.

Runnymede Commission on Anti-Semitism. (1994). *A very light sleeper: The persistence and dangers of anti-Semitism*. London: Runnymede Trust.

Saint-Blancat, C., & di Friedberg, O. S. (2005). Why are mosques a problem? Local politics and fear of Islam in Northern Italy. *Journal of Ethnic and Migration Studies, 31*(6), 1083–1104.

Salih, R. (2001). Confronting modernities Muslim women in Italy. *ISIM Newsletter, 7*, 2.

Salih, R. (2009). Muslim women, fragmented secularism and the construction of interconnected 'publics' in Italy. *Social Anthropology, 17*(4), 409–423.

Sardar, Z. (1995). Racism, identity and Muslims in the West. In S. Z. Abedin & Z. Sardar (Eds.), *Muslim minorities in the West* (pp. 1–17). London: Grey Seal.

Sayyid, S. (1997). *A fundamental fear: Eurocentrism and the emergence of Islamism*. London: Zed Books.

Sayyid, S. (2010). Thinking through Islamophobia. In S. Sayyid & A. Vakil (Eds.), *Thinking through Islamophobia: Global perspectives* (pp. 1–4). London: Hurst & Co.

Schwarz, T., & Cauchon, S. (2012). *Not in my backyard: 'Nordic' secularism and the rise of Islamophobia*. Annual Meeting of the Western Political Science Assn. March 22–24.

Scriver, P. (2004). Mosques, ghantowns and cameleers in the settlement history of colonial Australia. *Fabrications, 13*(2), 19–41.

Sheehan, P. (2009). Islamophobia is a fabrication. *Sydney Morning Herald*. Retrieved from https://www.smh.com.au/politics/federal/islamophobia-is-a-fabrication-20141112-9fjm.html?page=-1

Sheehi, S. (2011). *Islamophobia: The ideological campaign against Muslims*. New York: SCB Distributors.

Sherif, B. (2001). The ambiguity of boundaries in the fieldwork experience: Establishing rapport and negotiating insider/outsider status. *Qualitative Inquiry, 7*, 436–447.

Sherman, R. O. (2013). Imposter syndrome: When you feel like you're faking it. *American Nurse Today, 8*(5), 57–58.

Shyrock, A. (2010). *Islamophobia Islamophilia: Beyond the politics of enemy and friend*. Bloomington: Indiana University Press.

Sian, K. P. (2017). Surveillance, Islamophobia, and Sikh bodies in the war on terror. *Islamophobia Studies Journal, 4*(1), 37–52.

Spano, R. (2005). Potential sources of observer bias in police observational data. *Social Science Research, 34*, 591–617.

Spano, R. (2006). Observer behavior as a potential source of reactivity: Describing and quantifying observer effects in a large-scale observational study of police. *Sociological Methods & Research, 34*, 521–553.

Straw, J. (2006). I felt uneasy talking to someone I couldn't see. *Guardian*. Retrieved from https://www.theguardian.com/commentisfree/2006/oct/06/politics.uk

Stüssi, M. (2008). Banning of minarets: Addressing the validity of a controversial Swiss popular initiative. *Religion & Human Rights, 3*(2), 135–153.

Taras, R. (2012). *Xenophobia and Islamophobia in Europe*. Edinburgh: Edinburgh University Press.

Tarlo, E. (2007). Hijab in London: Metamorphosis, resonance and effects. *Journal of Material Culture, 12*(2), 131–156.

Tell MAMA. (2014). The resignation of Dr Chris Allen from the Cross Govt Working Group on anti-Muslim hatred is a wake up call. *Tell MAMA*. Retrieved from https://tellmamauk.org/resignation-dr-chris-allen-cross-govt-working-group-anti-muslim-hatred-wake-call/

Tell MAMA. (2017). *Beyond the incident: Outcomes for victims of anti-Muslim prejudice*. London: Faith Matters.

The Sun. (2019). Corrections and clarifications. *The Sun*. Retrieved from https://twitter.com/miqdaad/status/1166245228245860352/photo/1

Tufail, W. (2015). Rotherham, Rochdale, and the racialised threat of the 'Muslim Grooming Gang'. *International Journal for Crime, Justice and Social Democracy, 4*(3), 30–43.

Tufail, W., & Poynting, S. (2016). Muslim and dangerous: 'Grooming' and the politics of racialisation. In D. Pratt & R. Woodlock (Eds.), *Fear of Muslims?* (pp. 79–92). Cham: Springer.

Tyrer, D. (2013). *The politics of Islamophobia: Race, power and fantasy*. London: Pluto.

United Nations. (2008). *Report of the Special Rapporteur on contemporary forms of racism, racial discrimination, xenophobia and related intolerance, Doudou Diène, on the manifestations of defamation of religions and in particular on the serious implications of Islamophobia on the enjoyment of all rights*. New York: United Nations.

Ward, J. (2010). Sayeeda Warsi slammed by Islamic fundamentalists. *Daily Star*. Retrieved from http://www.dailystar.co.uk/news/latest-news/135481/Sayeeda-Warsi-slammed-by-Islamic-fundamentalists

Warsi, S. (2011). Sayeeda Warsi: University of Leicester Sir Sigmund Sternberg Lecture. *The Baroness Warsi*. Retrieved October 24, 2016, from http://sayeedawarsi.com/2011/01/20/university-of-leicester-sir-sigmundsternberg-lecture/

Weller, P. (2006). Addressing religious discrimination and Islamophobia: Muslims and liberal democracies. The case of the United Kingdom. *Journal of Islamic Studies, 17*, 295–325.

Weller, P., Feldman, A., & Purdam, K. (2001). *Religious discrimination in England & Wales (Home Office research study 220)*. London, UK: Home Office.

What Do They Know. (2012). Remit/membership of the Muslim Leadership Panel. *What Do They Know*. Retrieved from https://www.whatdotheyknow.com/request/136128/response/336750/attach/html/4/2011%2011%2014%20MLPmembers1.tif.html

Wieviorka, M. (1995). *The arena of racism*. London: Sage.

Wing, A. K., & Smith, M. N. (2005). Critical race feminism lifts the veil: Muslim women, France, and the headscarf ban. *UC Davis School of Law – Law Review, 39*, 743.

Wolfreys, J. (2018). *Republic of Islamophobia: The rise of respectable racism in France*. London: Hurst & Co.

Woodhead, L. (2010). *Religion or belief: Identifying issues and priorities*. Manchester, UK: Equality and Human Rights Commission.

Zemni, S. (2011). The shaping of Islam and Islamophobia in Belgium. *Race & Class, 53*(1), 28–44.

Zempi, I., & Awan, I. (2016). *Islamophobia: Lived experiences of online and offline victimisation*. Bristol: Policy Press.

Zempi, I., & Chakraborti, N. (2014). *Islamophobia, victimisation and the veil*. London: Palgrave Macmillan.

Index

C. Allen, *Reconfiguring Islamophobia*, Palgrave Hate Studies,
https://doi.org/10.1007/978-3-030-33047-7

The manufacturer's authorised representative in the EU is Springer Nature Customer Service Centre GmbH, Europaplatz 3, 69115 Heidelberg, Germany. If you have any concerns regarding our products, please contact ProductSafety@springernature.com

Printed and bound by CPI Group (UK) Ltd, Croydon, CR0 4YY
30/09/2026
02225466-0014